THE VEGETABLE BOOK

How to grow and cook your own vegetables

Terence Conran and Maria Kroll
Paintings by Faith Shannon

CRESCENT BOOKS

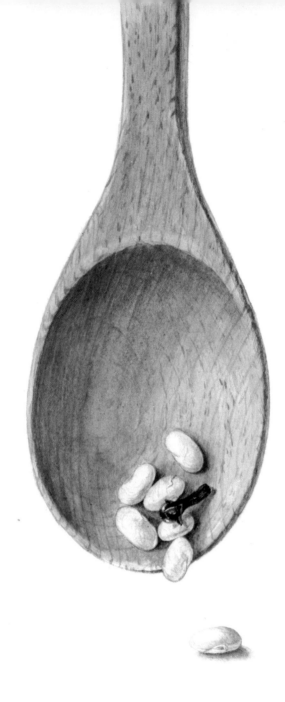

This edition first published by
Crescent Books
A division of Crown Publishers Inc.,
One Park Avenue, New York 10016

© 1976 Conran Ink

ISBN 0-517-44645-6

Printed in Hong Kong

Contents

To grow, cook and eat your own home-grown vegetables is one of the great pleasures in life.

Their cultivation does not require rolling acres – any well-planned plot can yield surprisingly large and varied crops. Even where there is no kitchen-garden proper, vegetables can be grown in selected spots, both for their usefulness and their beauty. Purplish cabbages look well when planted in front of cabbage roses; the tall silver foliage of artichokes makes a lovely background to a white or mixed flower-border; climbing beans, scarlet or purple flowered, are as pretty and fragrant as any sweet-pea and can handsomely climb up a trellis, even on a balcony; tomatoes and broad beans can flourish in large tubs.

Kitchen-gardens, where there *is* space for them, are fast becoming the focal point of interest: their owners find themselves showing visitors over rows of peas and beds of asparagus as they once showed them over the shrubs and flowers.

The new wave of enthusiasm for fresh vegetables is partly due to our increasing awareness of our dietary needs: vegetables, as any home-economist knows, supply us with vitamins and minerals and much protein; partly, because we realise that by growing our own we save money and gain enjoyment – the taste of freshly picked vegetables can be a revelation unequalled by the flavour of those bought in the shop or market. Partly, and we suspect that it is quite a large part, it is due to our desire for the simple things in life, for a degree of self-sufficiency, and even for the satisfaction that comes with having a proper sense of the seasons. Stout winter vegetables warm and cheer us by supplying interior central heating when the cold weather comes along, and although some of the ubiquitous frozen vegetables are both good and convenient, we long for the pleasure of eating their tender young counterparts fresh from the garden.

Carrots, pulled out of the soil before they have grown into marketable giants, plunged into boiling water for a very few minutes, and dished up glistening with fresh butter and speckled with your own chopped parsley, put bought carrots to shame. Asparagus, cut and eaten within the hour are a revelation of delicate flavour. Bought broad beans are virtually unobtainable at their best, which is when they are very young, each kernel a delicate emerald green; even to make them emerge from their foam-lined pods is a pleasure when they are picked in this state.

Vegetables, naturally, deserve as much care in the kitchen as in the garden: the recipes given here are all designed to get the very best out of them, and to heighten your enjoyment of the best food from the earth.

Terence Conran

Marvels can be performed in kitchen and garden with the very minimum of equipment. Greed and natural green fingers are usually half the battle, but for the other half a sensible arsenal, here divided into a *batterie de cuisine* and a *batterie de jardin*, can be a great help.

Obviously, no particularly esoteric equipment is needed for vegetable cookery. Commonsense suggests that the more good cook's knives you own, the more helpers will be able to lend a hand with scraping, peeling and chopping. Commonsense also suggests that a special board, reserved for onions and garlic only, is a good idea, because a quick wipe with a moist cloth does not generally get rid of the smell, and you may need the board for other things before it is properly aired.

A mandoline and a mouli-légumes make a real difference to salads and soups, and are therefore basic gadgets; all others – the various peelers, corers, juice extractors, scoops and slicers – are a matter of personal taste. Things like ring moulds, timbales, soufflé and gratin dishes come into their own in vegetable cookery, and an essential part of the comfort of soup lies in ladling it out at the table from a pot-bellied soup tureen.

Besides the things illustrated you will need

several saucepans ● omelette pan ● frying pan ● preserving pan ● pie dishes ● gratin dishes ● cocottes ● sauté pans ● oval terrine ● 1 small thick pan for making sauce ● deep frying pan with a basket ● double boiler ● tin pie plates ● demi-lune chopper ● masher ● large metal spoon ● perforated spoon ● mincer ● mixer ● liquidizer ● mouli-parsmint ● salad shaker ● fine sieve ● juice extractor ● measuring jug ● glass storage jars

Gardening equipment can also be divided into essentials and things which are simply nice to have. Buy the very best basic tools you can afford. Stainless steel repays the extra expense by being lighter and easier to use than any other metal. Earth will not cling to it and, even if your soil is heavy, a stainless steel spade will cut through it like butter. The same goes for the garden fork, the hoe and even for the small hand tools. In the case of trowels and little forks which deal with smaller loads of soil, the non-stick aspect is not so vital, but they and all other garden tools should be well scraped and wiped before they are put away.

What you will need will be dictated by the area you mean to cultivate. Windowsill and terrace gardeners obviously need neither spades nor clogs, but miniature trowels and hand forks designed for use with flowerpots are more efficient than kitchen spoons. But whether you are engaging on large- or small-scale gardening, there is something to be said for starting with the simple tools and adding to the collection as you go along.

Besides the equipment illustrated you will need

gardening apron or smock; gardening gloves and gum boots ● spray or syringe ● secateurs and pruning scissors ● cloches, Dutch lights or cold frames ● box for seed packets ● seed boxes ● various boxes for storage; sacks; bamboo canes ● trug or large basket ● Large-scale gardeners will also need a length of hosepipe, a sprinkler and a wheelbarrow. ● The gardener without a garden will only need pots, a trowel, seed boxes, hand fork, scissors and canes for staking climbers.

Batteries

The utensils you will need most often for preparing vegetable dishes

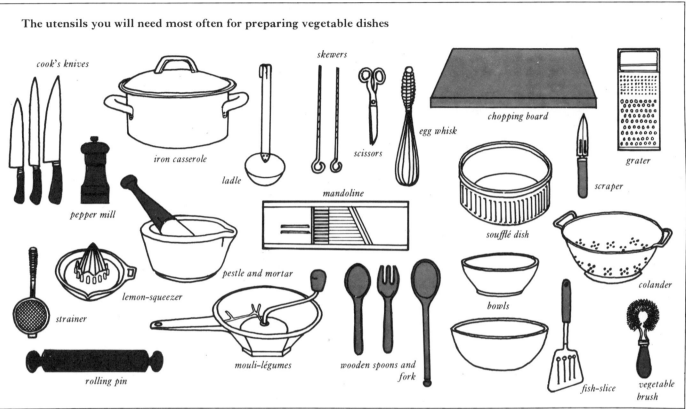

cook's knives

iron casserole

pepper mill

ladle

skewers

scissors

egg whisk

chopping board

grater

scraper

mandoline

soufflé dish

colander

pestle and mortar

lemon-squeezer

strainer

bowls

fish-slice

vegetable brush

rolling pin

mouli-légumes

wooden spoons and fork

Gardening things you will not want to be without

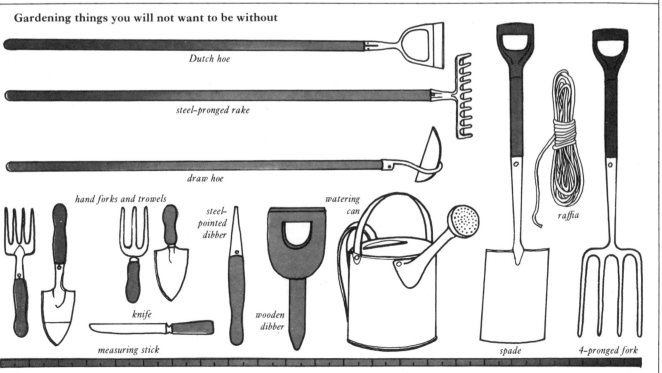

Dutch hoe

steel-pronged rake

draw hoe

hand forks and trowels

steel-pointed dibber

watering can

raffia

knife

wooden dibber

measuring stick

spade

4-pronged fork

BUDS & STEMS

Artichoke *Cynara scolymus*

This spectacular globe is the bud of a glorified thistle, the cardoon, which used to grow wild in many parts of the world. Cultivated 'from his wildnesse to serve unto the use of the mouth', the artichoke became 'Prince of dainties'. No banquet was complete without it. Along with swans, ibises, egrets and three bustards in full feather, it appeared at Catherine de Medici's wedding feast. (The bride ate too much which almost ruined the nuptials.)

Henry VIII's menu included a dish of artichokes and boiled sparrows as a special delicacy, but from the seventeenth century onwards artichokes were enjoyed by prince and commoner alike. They were also popular, it seems, with mice and moles; gardeners were advised to train weasels to hunt over their artichoke beds.

ARTICHOKE *Cynara scolymus*

Artichokes no longer form an inevitable part of the kitchen garden, but they are easy to grow and a treat to eat. They give a sense of special occasion, and, served as starters at a dinner-party, make marvellous ice-breakers; no one can be pompous for long while getting to grips with this excellent vegetable. It contains vitamin B and C. A boon to slimmers,

a heart when cooked has barely 2 calories – sadly without butter. Unfortunately, artichokes destroy the flavour of wine, so serve a good claret with the main course.

If you serve artichokes as a first course, plan so that what follows is not dependent on split-second timing. You cannot be sure just how long people will take to pull out the scaly leaves one by one so that the fleshy base, dipped into a sauce, can be enjoyed; or to remove the choke (the central hairy thatch) to reach the heart or bottom, the *fond d'artichaut*. This, the best bit, is eaten with knife and fork.

Basic treatment

For artichokes to be served with a sauce, preparation is simple. Pick them long-stemmed. If they have to lie about in a warm kitchen, put them into water as you would a bunch of flowers. Then wash them under running water and snap off the tough, small leaves at the bottom. The tips of the main leaves can be trimmed with the scissors, or left alone. Some people prefer to trim off the top third of the globe, where the leaves are less fleshy, with a stainless steel knife, and to remove the choke by scraping and scooping with a spoon. As artichokes discolour easily, rub a lemon over the cut areas. Break off the artichoke stems so that the fibrous strings can be pulled out,

6

trim the base so that they can sit squarely on the plate. Bring a huge pan of salted water to the boil and throw them in. Boil for 25–35 minutes according to size and freshness. Tug at a lower leaf; when it comes away easily, it is ready.

Drain artichokes, head down, giving them a little squeeze to get rid of any liquid caught in the interior. Prod them back into shape before you serve them either hot with Hollandaise or Mousseline sauce, or butter; or cold, with a Vinaigrette, mayonnaise, or *sauce verte*.

It must not be thought that artichokes are useful only as starters. Huge ones, filled with a variety of stuffings, make interesting and satisfying main courses. The little spiky ones with unrewarding outer leaves have delicious hearts to be prepared *à la grecque*, as a salad.

Some of the classic steaks of French *haute cuisine* need artichokes for their garnish. Tournedos Henri IV are accompanied by little *fonds d'artichaut* filled with Béarnaise sauce and a sliver of truffle. The garnish of tournedos Clamart and Choron consists of artichoke hearts, simmered in butter and filled with tiny green peas, or a purée of larger ones, or asparagus tips. These garnishes go just as nicely with other small cuts of meat; artichokes have a special affinity with veal. And although Henri IV's truffles – along with cockscombs that gourmets expect with artichoke-topped tournedos Marguéry – are unlikely to loom large in our store cupboards, all these combinations can make memorable courses.

Stuffed artichokes à la barigoule (*for 6*)

6 artichokes, chokes removed	*for the stuffing:*
6 rashers rindless bacon	6 bacon rashers
olive oil	3 onions; 12 mushrooms
1 large onion	2 slices stale white bread
1 large clove garlic	5–6 tablespoons stock or water
2 medium-sized carrots	parsley; garlic; nutmeg
1 glass white wine	2 egg yolks; salt; pepper

Make the stuffing by chopping the bacon and the onions, frying them together until they start to brown, then adding the chopped mushrooms, the bread soaked in water, squeezed dry and crumbled, the stock, seasoning, nutmeg, finely chopped garlic and parsley. Remove from the heat and stir in the egg yolks.

Stuff the hollow centres of your artichokes with the mixture. Cover each artichoke with a rasher of bacon and tie. In the bottom of a fireproof casserole put 3 tablespoons olive oil, a chopped onion, the garlic and the chopped carrots. Put the casserole over a brisk heat, soften the vegetables, then add a glass of white wine and put in the artichokes. Season, and sprinkle with a little more oil. Add 2 whole cloves of garlic and half a glass of water. Cover and simmer until the artichokes are tender (they will take about 1 hour). Serve hot with the liquid and vegetables from the casserole.

An easier way to prepare stuffed artichokes is to boil them in salted water until the choke can be removed easily.

Then fill them with any of the following: creamed spinach, chopped cooked chicken bound in a white sauce; chicken-livers, chopped and sautéed with onion.

Ham and mushroom stuffing

For each artichoke you will need a slice of ham, 1 medium-sized mushroom, and 1 teaspoonful of chopped onion. Colour the onion and the finely chopped mushroom slightly in butter, add a sprinkling of flour to make a brown roux, and moisten with water, or stock, until the sauce has the consistency of thick cream. Season, add the chopped ham, spoon into the artichoke, sprinkle with fresh breadcrumbs and dot with butter. Bake for 10 minutes in a greased, fireproof dish.

How to grow globe artichokes

They are usually grown from rooted offsets or suckers. Plant in late spring, in an airy position and well-drained soil, when they are about 9in (23cm) tall. You can also grow them from seed, under glass in early spring in boxes or in the open in late spring. In fine weather you can get edible heads that year, but usually in the following season. Rich soil and a lot of watering in dry weather give succulent heads. Old stems and decaying leaves should be removed and suckers cut at the end of the season. Always cut the heads before the purple petals show; this gives others a chance to develop. 3 or 4 main shoots to a plant will give good heads. Wood ash and seaweed are appreciated and so is well-composted soil. Plants can stay in the same place for 2 to 3 years; then they become exhausted, and you start again from the beginning.

1. Plants grown from seed in pots or boxes, early

2. Plants or suckers are planted firmly 1yd (1m) apart

3. Cut large heads when ripe. Remove very small ones

4. Flower heads are beautiful for cutting

Artichoke croquettes

These make a good light meal with cold ham. The flesh scraped from the bottom of artichoke leaves, and the bottoms, are passed through a sieve, bound with a thick Béchamel sauce, shaped into thumb-sized croquettes, breadcrumbed and fried in butter or oil.

Artichokes à la greque

Remove all spiky bits. The hearts – i.e. all the edible parts, are cooked in a mixture of olive oil and lemon juice. Use twice as much oil as lemon, and let the liquid just cover the vegetables. Add some crushed peppercorns and coriander seeds. The artichoke hearts will be ready after they have simmered for about 30 minutes, and should be allowed to cool in the liquid. Decant them into a serving dish and chill them well.

CARDOON *Cynara cardunculus*

This very good vegetable, sometimes called chard in the USA, must be earthed up for blanching like celery. Only the stalks are edible. It is rarely found in gardens, but, being a more spiny version of its first cousin the artichoke, it is good to eat. Incidentally, cardoon recipes can apply just as well to artichoke stalks – which is cheering to gardeners because there is so much of that to each bud.

Basic treatment

The outer leaves and the stringy outer layers are pared away. Like artichokes, cardoons blacken when exposed to air, so plunge them into acidulated water – or quickly chop them into finger lengths – and boil in salted water. Dish up with butter and chopped parsley, or put them into a fireproof dish, mask them with a Béchamel sauce, generously sprinkle with grated cheese and dot with butter, and brown in the oven.

Cardoons with peas

Put the trimmed stalks in a stew-pan containing some hot oil. Season with salt and pepper. Cover and cook for about 10 minutes. Then, to the same weight as the trimmed cardoons (or artichoke stalks), add small green peas and a head of lettuce cut into coarse strips. Cover tightly, and cook gently for 20 minutes without moistening. The lettuce should yield enough liquid to prevent burning. If extra moisture *is* needed, add it in very small amounts; the charm of this dish depends on the concentrated flavour.

Cardoons Provençal

Start this dish, which is particularly good with braised lamb, by cooking the trimmed cardoons in hot oil as in the preceding recipe, but instead of using peas, add first 2 cloves of crushed garlic, and when this has had time to develop its aroma in the oil, about 8 skinned, roughly chopped tomatoes. Stir them about a bit, and cook, hermetically sealed, for about 30 minutes.

ASPARAGUS *Asparagus officinalis*

Asparagus has always had a good press. From the Ancients onwards, people have spoken well of what an English seventeenth-century cookery book describes as 'that delicate fruite and wholesome for everiebodie, and especially when it is thicke, tender and sweete, and not verie much boiled.' Thickness came with cultivation, but the very thin sort – often called 'sprue' or 'grass' – is not to be despised. Scraggy shoots, growing wild in temperate zones, used to be relished wherever they poked out their heads from the sandy soil in which they thrive: even a thorny variety growing in Spain. When the gourmets and the market-gardeners of the world got busy, three main varieties eventually emerged: white ones

---

How to grow asparagus

Asparagus beds are commonly 5ft (1·5m) wide. They are deeply dug and enriched with compost. Three-year old roots or crowns go into the earth as soon as they arrive from the nursery; do not let them wait about – they languish and sometimes die. (If you sow seed, do it in rows 12in (30cm) apart, plant out 12 months hence; cut no spears for 3 years.) Water very frequently. Asparagus will pop up all over the place in early summer. Even with three-year old plants, cut only for 6 weeks all lengths and thickness, later you can cut for 8 weeks without harming the plants. Then let them make fern to feed the roots. Do not cut this until it is yellow, but before the berries form.

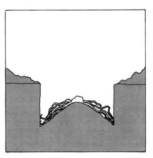

1. Put in spider-like roots, cover with fine soil

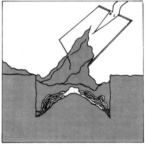

2. Gradually fill the asparagus trench over the summer

3. Cut the spears getting your sharp, broad knife well below the soil

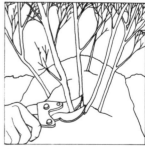

4. Cut down fern before the red berries appear

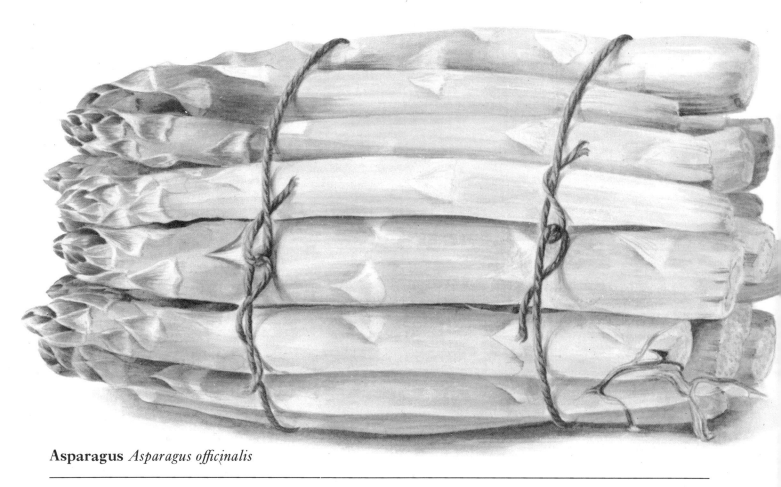

Asparagus *Asparagus officinalis*

with ivory tips; violet-tinted ones, and those that are green all over. Because of the shortness of the season and the large amount of space that needs to be devoted to it, asparagus became an expensive delicacy. Dishes garnished with asparagus tips are called *à la princesse*, and reflect their grandeur. So fond of them was Louis XIV that his gardeners devised a way to grow them in special frames from spring to December. What with imported and canned, not to mention frozen asparagus, it can now, theoretically, be enjoyed all the year round. But there is literally *nothing* to beat the flavour of your own asparagus, fat or thin, brought in from the garden and dropped, at once, into a waiting pan of boiling water for 4–7 minutes. Asparagus, containing vitamins A, B, and C, is very low in calories, less than 25 a helping. (Butter, of course, again counts extra.)

Basic treatment

Asparagus gathered before it is needed will keep crisp in the vegetable compartment of a refrigerator. If you have to keep them even in a cool larder, stand them, like flowers, in a jar with an inch or so of water. Thick asparagus with a woody base should be pared (downwards) with the sharpest possible cook's knife. If the base still feels woody, trim it off. Classically, stem asparagus is tied into bundles, heads together, and stood shoulder high in boiling salted water in a special pan. The idea is to let the delicate heads steam while the stems cook. But it is possible to cook stem asparagus in an ordinary pan by leaning the vegetables untied, against the side. By the time that the stems have cooked in salted water for about 5 minutes, they will have become pliable enough for the whole asparagus, tips and all, to be eased into the pot. Finish cooking until they are soft but not limp; 10 minutes or so should do it (cooking time depends on freshness and thickness). Sprue, generally too thin for paring, should simply be divested of all woody parts. (Do not make the mistake of thinking that thin shoots will grow thicker if you leave them in the soil. They become longer, but no fatter, and the tips will open up or grow mushy, depending on the weather.)

Hot stem asparagus

Stem asparagus, the great treat of the early summer, is eaten hot or cold, and needs appropriate dips. Hot, asparagus is nice with butter, melted, with an addition of a few drops of lemon juice or with nut-brown butter in which breadcrumbs have been browned. Warm – in most cases asparagus should be not piping hot, but on the tepid side – it is eaten with a Hollandaise or Mousseline sauce. *Beurre blanc*, tricky to make, is a wonderful accompaniment; or, more simply, butter that has been whipped up with a fork until it is fluffy but not oily. Served with thinly sliced boiled ham, asparagus with whipped butter makes a good, light, summer lunch. To serve asparagus *à la flamande* means halved hard-boiled eggs arranged around a dish of hot asparagus, with bread-crumb-butter dished up separately. Eaters themselves mix the egg and sauce on their plate before dipping. If you want to dish asparagus up *à la polonaise*, sprinkle the tips with chopped hard-boiled egg, and serve with Noisette butter.

Cold stem asparagus

Cold asparagus responds marvellously to mayonnaise, or can come to the table with a garlic-free French dressing, which makes it into a sort of salad.

Asparagus rolls (*for 4*)

1½lb (675g) asparagus	1½oz (½ cup; 35g) flour
1 pint (½l; 2 cups) water	grated Parmesan cheese
6 bread rolls	salt, pepper
5½oz (¾ cup; 140g) butter	3 tablespoons cream

Trim and cook the asparagus in the water and drain it saving the liquid. Cut the rolls in half and scoop out the crumbs. Fry the crusts in butter until golden-brown on both sides. Meanwhile, make a smooth sauce with the remaining butter, the flour and three-quarters of the liquid, season well and flavour it lightly with grated cheese. (You are not making cheese sauce; the flavour of the cheese should be almost undetectable.) Lastly, beat in the cream. Cut the tender green parts of the asparagus into 1½in (4cm) pieces, throwing away the tough parts of the stalk. Put the asparagus tips and stems into the sauce, heat through thoroughly and pour the mixture into the crisp, browned rolls, letting it flow over the sides. Serve 2 or 3 halves of roll to each person. The crumbs of the rolls can be toasted and used to make good breadcrumbs.

Asparagus soup

Cut about ½lb (225g) trimmed asparagus (sprue will do well, it would be a pity to cut up thick spears), into mouth-sized pieces. Boil briskly in 2 pints of salt water. Make a white roux in another saucepan, and, gradually add the liquid. Simmer until the soup has reached the consistency you like, and toss in the cooked asparagus. Heat through, and at the last moment add a good dash of thick cream, which should not be stirred in but merely 'drawn' across the surface. For cream of asparagus soup, you would sieve, mouli or liquefy all but the tips of the vegetables; and for a gala version, you would mix 1 or 2 egg yolks with a dash of cream or the top of the milk, and reheat the soup without allowing it to come to the boil, before adding some thick cream as a finishing touch.

Asparagus with feather-light egg gnocchi

Prepare the asparagus, allowing about 6 spears per head, as above. Cover with a mixture of salted water and milk and boil. When the asparagus is done, drain and make a white sauce with the liquid. While this bubbles, prepare the gnocchi:

For these you need 1 egg (white and yolk separated). 3 tablespoons of self-raising flour. A little milk. A walnut of butter, and salt. Put the egg white in a cup and fill to the brim with milk. Pour into a small saucepan, together with the butter and the salt. Then add the flour, and, over gentle heat, stir until the mixture eventually forms a smooth ball. Draw off the heat, vigorously beat in the egg yolk and, using a teaspoon dipped in cold water, spoon off a trial lump the size of a new potato and drop it into the bubbling sauce. It will sink below the surface, but will soon come bobbing up again looking like a little feather bed. Lift out carefully with a perforated spoon, test to see whether it is cooked through; if not, return to the liquid until it feels light and looks opaque all through. Time this, and cook the rest of the gnocchi, a few at a time, accordingly. Serves 2 or 3 people.

Asparagus omelette

Asparagus makes a particularly successful omelette filling. There is the added advantage that even with quite few vegetables, you can still produce an asparagus dish worthy of the name. Cut the spears small (especially if you have a few green peas with which to mix them). Cook in the usual way, reserving the tips for garnish. Drain and keep warm. Cook the omelette, having been careful not to overbeat the eggs. Then put the asparagus onto one half of the glistening, fluffy surface, dot with a bit of fresh butter, fold the omelette so that the asparagus is covered, and strew with the tips. For another very good version, bed the asparagus in a smooth stiff white sauce, made with the cooking liquid, and fill the omelette with the mixture.

Asparagus au four

A very good way of using left-over cooked asparagus, is to place it in layers in a well-buttered fireproof dish, having trimmed away any inedible parts. Cover the top halves with a thick Mornay sauce, sprinkled with grated cheese and dotted with butter, and cover the bottom portion with foil, and brown. Or simply sprinkle the whole lot with cheese, shaking the dish a little so that the cheese nestles between the stalks, pour a little melted butter over the lot, and gently brown.

Drinks-time asparagus

Everyone has met asparagus tips individually rolled into fresh, thin slices of buttered brown bread.

A different way of using sprue is to cut the spears into pea-sized pieces, and to cook them in a minimum of water acidulated with a few drops of lemon juice. The moisture should have practically evaporated by the time they are cooked. Then add a little butter so that the asparagus glistens, and heap it into round or boat-shaped pastry shells, baked blind beforehand.

ROOTS

Root vegetables, the wild-growing ancestors of our parsnips, carrots, turnips and beets, have been eaten with various degrees of enthusiasm since the beginning of time. Highly nutritious, they formed the staple part of our forebears' diet. In neolithic times, leaf-wrapped assortments were roasted in hot ashes, but civilization marched on, and with it sophistication in cookery. The Romans rather despised roots, hardly stooping to use them as flavouring agents for their dishes of larks' tongues and ostrich brains. The French despise parsnips still, few of their cookery books deign to mention them at all. Turnips, carrots and beetroot, however, featured in French Renaissance feasts. Carved into grotesque shapes, they accompanied showily dressed roasts, but as decoration only. In the eighteenth century, they came into their own again. The Duc de Richelieu, gentleman of goodness knows how many bedchambers – who obviously needed a fortifying diet – pronounced 'beef and roots' the prettiest supper in the world. (No connection, however, with *carottes rapées*.)

Less concerned with deliciousness, and more with remedial properties, were the old herbals: 'The roote of the parsenep hanged on the necke doth helpe the swelling of the throte,' says a sixteenth-century herbalist. Beetroot juice, snuffed up the nose, was believed to purge the brain, while fresh beet leaves were applied to the head 'against the shedding of the haire'. Carrots, boiled, were used as a cure for asthma in the eighteenth century. During the Second World War, the British were wooed into eating carrots because Air Force pilots, by consuming quantities, had apparently been enabled to see in the dark. However, later it turned out that Radar, not carrots, had been responsible for Allied night-time successes, and the nation thankfully took carrot jam and carrot pudding off the menu, concentrating instead on root vegetables in their proper place.

Parsnip
Pastinaca sativa

PARSNIP *Pastinaca sativa*

The parsnip contains some vitamin B and C, also calcium and iron; fairly high in carbohydrates, and therefore calories, about 100 calories a helping.

The nineteenth-century doyenne of all cookery writers, Eliza Acton, recommends her recipe for parsnip soup 'particularly to those who like the peculiar flavour of this vegetable.' Fair enough: perhaps the haunting memory of greyish, mashed nursery horrors is to blame for the small esteem in which parsnips are traditionally held. Even a seventeenth-century recommender felt moved to observe that the parsnip is '. . . the best food for tame rabets and makes them sweet.'

However, parsnips are well worth the eating, especially if they have been touched by a frost or two, although by then they will no longer be in their first youth. So it is important to remove the core, which even in young parsnips is almost flavourless, and in aged ones has turned to wood.

Basic treatment

Cut off the top and roots, peel or scrape and cut lengthways. After taking out the core, cut into pieces suitable for your dish. To boil, allow about 20 minutes in salted water. Steaming will take 35 to 40 minutes. Parsnips go well with roast lamb and pork (and, of course, rabbit). They are especially nice when they are parboiled for about 5 minutes and placed in the roasting tin with the joint, either surrounding it or, better still, placed directly underneath the meat to catch the juices. They do, however, make perfectly good dishes in their own right. Fine words, we are told, will not butter them; why parsnips should be singled out as candidates for lavish buttering is a mystery, since what John Evelyn, another seventeenth-century partisan of the parsnip, calls 'their oyntment-like' consistency needs little further emulsifying.

Parsnip soup (*for 4*)

Gently stew 2lb (900g) parsnips in melted butter for 10 minutes. Then add enough stock to cover them, and let them boil briskly for 20 minutes. Sieve, add more of the stock, and reduce by half, skimming every now and then. Put in salt and pepper to taste and add cream after the soup has stopped boiling. Serve with croûtons.

Parsnip salad

John Evelyn writes 'The parsnep, first boil'd is of it self a Winter Sallet, eaten with oyl, vinegar is by some thought more nourishing than the turnep.' Another parsnip salad, also called 'poor man's lobster salad' requires halved cooked parsnips, thinly sliced after cooling. These are dressed in a stiff sharp mayonnaise, prepared with lemon rather than vinegar. The result, vaguely reminiscent of lobster salad in consistency if not in taste, makes a good hors d'oeuvre.

Fried parsnips (*for 4*)

1lb (450g) parsnips	nutmeg or mace
butter	salt
1 egg, beaten	flour

Cooked and drained parsnips are mashed with a walnut of butter and half of the beaten egg, a pinch of nutmeg or mace, and one of salt, and formed into stubby rolls about the length and circumference of a thumb. Gently rolled first in the remaining egg and then in flour, they will keep their shape; it helps to put them in the refrigerator for a little while before frying. They can be crisply deep-fried, but are equally nice if they are simply sautéed in the frying pan; good with roast or braised meat.

Another method is to cut raw parsnips into sticks the size of chipped potatoes and to deep-fry them. Or quartered parsnips can be parboiled, breadcrumbed, and shallow-fried to a golden brown.

How to grow parsnips

Parsnips are sown as early as possible in the spring in well-dug, and un-stoney soil. To get a really long root it is a good idea to bore holes in the soil 2–3ft (60–90cm) deep and about 3in (8cm) across at the top. Fill the holes with potting compost, and sow three seeds at the top of each, thinning down to one later. Seeds are slow to germinate, so intercrop with radish or lettuce seeds – these will come up first and show you where the row is, and make hoeing less of a danger.

1. Sow in drills, 12in (30cm) apart, in holes 10in (25cm) apart made with a stick

2. Fill in with compost or sifted soil, sow 3–4 seeds 1in (2·5cm) deep and cover with more fine soil

3. Thin to 1 when seedlings are large enough to handle

4. Lift only as needed; parsnips improve with frost

Parsnip gratin

In a well-buttered pie-dish, place alternate layers of raw, sliced parsnips, sliced tomatoes and a sprinkling of grated cheese dotted with butter. (Any hard cheese will do.) End with a layer of parsnips about a finger's width from the top of the dish. Then make a layer of white breadcrumbs. It is this that, strictly speaking, constitutes the gratin or upper crust, and not the grated cheese which should now be added in a generous top sprinkling, then dotted with more butter. Cook in a slow oven; an excellent nourishing main course. Serve with a crisp salad made of lettuce and watercress in equal parts.

Parsnip flan

A long way removed from the wartime puddings earlier discussed is this very pretty country dish, which uses the sweetness of parsnips to good advantage.
Boil and drain some parsnips and press them through a sieve. To about 1 pint (½l; 2 cups) of this golden mush add 1 tablespoon of honey, a strong dash of ginger and a pinch of spice. Beat in the golden grated rind and juice of 2 lemons and the yolk of 1 egg (reserving the white). Line a flan tin with thin shortcrust pastry and fill it with the mixture. Make a lattice across the flan with the cut trimmings and bake until golden-brown. Pile the beaten egg white (sweetened and flavoured with a little of the lemon rind) in a ring round the edge and return the flan to the cool oven to set. Serve cold, garnished with primroses at the crossings of the lattice.

Parsnip wine

Pale golden homemade parsnip wine, like wine of cowslips, elderberries or elderberry flowers, is part of the country tradition, and deserves to be revived. There is a lot of practical wine-making equipment about, but basically, especially for smallish quantities, all that is needed are 2 large vessels – plastic or stoneware, not metal – cheese-cloth, clean bottles and new corks, a tray to catch the overspill during the fermenting process, a funnel and a long wooden spoon. Wine-making yeast and the yeast nutrient that is used with it are readily available. These have largely taken the place of the bread-making yeast used in former days, because they are more foolproof and do not adversely affect the flavour of the wine.

To make parsnip wine, scrub and scrape 7lb (3·15kg) parsnips, slice them and boil in 12 pints (6·25l) water until they are tender (but don't let them go mushy, otherwise the wine will never be clear). You can boil the parsnip pieces in half the water and add the rest, warm, later. Tie a cloth or jelly bag over a large earthenware jar or a plastic bucket and strain the liquid through; this will take some time but do not squeeze or press the pieces or the wine will be cloudy. Measure the liquid and add 3lb (1·35kg) of white sugar to 8 pints (4·5l) and the juice of 2 lemons. Bring to the boil and simmer for 45 minutes, then pour the liquid into the jar or

bucket. When the wine has cooled to lukewarm, add approximately ¾ tablespoon of wine-making yeast and the yeast nutrient. Cover well with a cloth and a lid, and leave in a warm place for 10 days, stirring well every day. Strain into a cask or fermenting jar with an air lock and leave for 6 months or more in a cooler place. The wine will by then be clear. Syphon the wine into clean bottles or jars and keep for a further 6 months, when it should be delicious, and even better the following year.

SALSIFY *Tragopogon porrifolius*

Salsify is sown in late spring about 1in (2·5cm) deep in drills 12in (30cm) apart, and should be thinned to 8in (20cm). Salsify is also called the oyster plant, or vegetable oyster – for what reason it is impossible to say, for its flavour is unlike that of fish, flesh or any other vegetable. It has an elegant, special flavour and is particularly good with plain boiled chicken. Salsify need a long growing season, about 7 months from sowing to reaping. The true salsify is black-skinned and white-fleshed, but some varieties have pale skins. None should be peeled, but merely scraped before they go into the pot. Salsify is low on calories (under 30 in a large helping).

Basic treatment

Plunge the scraped roots, topped and tailed, and cut into thumb-length chunks, into acidulated water to preserve their creamy whiteness. Cook in boiling salted water until they are done, which may take up to an hour depending on the age and freshness of the vegetable.

Any recipe calling for Jerusalem artichokes will accept salsify as a worthy substitute. The cooked vegetables are generally eaten with a variety of sauces. Mask them in Béchamel sauce – to which a little cream has been added as a final touch – for their flavour to be at its most poignant; or arrange them in a fireproof dish, cover with a Mornay sauce, pour some melted butter over the top and sprinkle with grated Parmesan cheese and brown. Eat them *au beurre* – the butter can be nut-brown, or simply melted – or gently sauté them and serve with chopped herbs. For salsify salad, pour an oil and lemon dressing over the cooled, cooked vegetables, and again sprinkle with finely chopped herbs.

HAMBURG PARSLEY
Carum petroselinum fusiformis

This useful root, also called parsnip or turnip-rooted parsley, is virtually never found in shops, and rarely in gardens. It is well worth growing for its smooth conical roots. It is sown in spring in well-cultivated ground in drills 18in (45cm) apart, and thinned to 9in (24cm) apart.

Its flavour is somewhere between the taste of celery and parsley, and its nutrients are similar to those of the parsnip.

It is less sweet, so there are fewer calories to the helping.

Hamburg parsley is invaluable as a soup vegetable, making the broth of boiled chicken or boiled beef taste more strongly of itself. The thinnings, tender miniature roots, can be tossed in a saucepan with baby carrots and dished up with butter making a delicious vegetable mixture.

CARROT *Daucus carota*

A carrot a day will provide the average daily requirement of vitamin A. It also contains vitamins B, C and E, and 1 boiled carrot will yield about 20 calories.

A dish of young carrots, fast-boiled in salted water, sprinkled with parsley and chives and served with fresh butter is one of the best things in the world to eat. Plain-boiled beef, carrots and dumplings have a natural affinity, and carrots together with onions and celery, form the base of the classical *bouillons* and broths. Stews, whether beef, veal or lamb are nicer and go further if carrots are added halfway through. In French cuisine, anything called *à la Crécy* and *Vichy* usually contains carrots. Roasts become *à la flamande* if they arrive surrounded by little mounds of cabbage alternating with turnips and carrots.

Many different varieties of carrots, large, small, tapering, stubby, spherical, and ranging in colour from palest apricot to bright red, are cultivated all over the world.

The larger varieties are most suitable for winter storage and, although a little less delicate in flavour, do well for the hefty country dishes that keep us warm in winter.

Basic treatment

Whenever possible, do not pare or even scrape carrots. Their flavour, and the vitamins and minerals they contain, are found directly under the surface. Simply scrub and top and tail the vegetables. Then parboil them, hold them under the cold tap, and slip them out of their skins: Leave small carrots whole. Larger ones are sliced, cut into cubes or lengthways, according to the dish that is in preparation. Their cooking time will depend on their age; baby carrots, freshly picked, will take no more than 3 minutes (and should simply be reheated after they have been stripped), carrots from the winter store will take up to 30 minutes. If you find that the centres of old carrots have turned woody, cut them out. Cooked carrots should be neither mushy nor crunchy.

Carrot soup (*for 4*)

This pureed soup is also called Potage Crécy. The name may originate from the French town in the area where the finest carrots grow.

For this soup you need about 1lb (450g) of carrots, 3 table-spoons of butter, 2 tablespoons of chopped onion, 2 pints (1¼l; 4 cups) of stock or water, a pinch of salt, a lump of sugar and 3 tablespoons of rice (or the equivalent of stale white bread with the crusts removed). Cut the carrots into thin slices and gently cook them in half the butter, together with the onions. When they are tender, add the liquid and the rice or bread. Simmer for 20 minutes, then pass them through a sieve, adding more liquid if the purée is too stiff. Reheat with the rest of the butter and serve with golden croûtons.

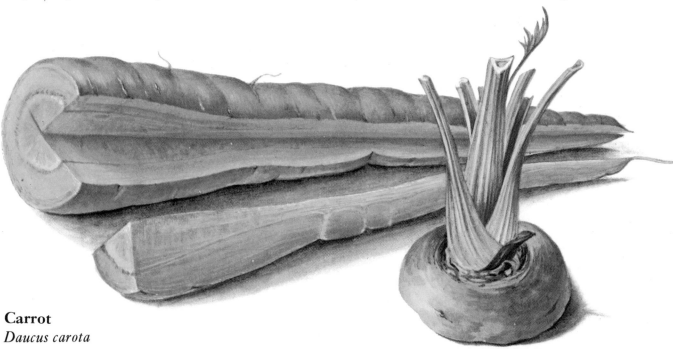

Carrot
Daucus carota

Carrot and cream soup (*for 4*)

2 bunches new carrots	salt
3 new potatoes	1½ pints (1l; 3 cups) creamy
1 dozen baby silver onions	milk
3 or 4 sprigs parsley	6 tablespoons cream

Cut up the carrots and potatoes, and roughly chop the little onions. Put the vegetables in a pan and cover them with cold water. Add salt and parsley, and cook until all the vegetables are tender, about 25 minutes. Sieve finely or liquidize, and add the milk. Add more salt if necessary. Eat hot or cold with 2 tablespoons of cream added to each helping at the last minute. The soup is a beautiful golden colour, flecked here and there with green.

Carrottes rapées

This way of serving carrots is an essential part of what the French call *crudités* – an assortment of raw vegetables, all served separately. For the carrot part, finely shred on a mandoline 2 or 3 good carrots. Dress them in a Vinaigrette for which you have used white wine vinegar, olive oil, a little mustard and no sugar (the carrots themselves are sweet enough). Do not heap the carrots on a lettuce leaf – it adds nothing by way of texture and rather spoils the flavour; no genuine French restaurant would dream of doing such a thing. Some children like carrots prepared in this fashion as a sandwich filling – it's almost as sweet as jam.

Carrots in marinade

For a cold meal of meat or fish, to be served with mixed salads, marinated carrots are more interesting than shredded ones.
To prepare a bland marinade, pour into a pan 1 glass of white wine with an equal quantity of water and 1 tablespoon of white wine vinegar. Add 1 crushed clove of garlic, a pinch of salt and pepper, 1 bay leaf and 4 tablespoons of oil. For a stronger marinade, use more vinegar and less water. Bring to the boil, toss in the carrots (cut into thin strips or rings) and cook briskly for about 7 minutes. This is a dish in which there should be a hint of the raw vegetable. Let the carrots cook in the liquid. If you like the flavour, mix some of the marinade with 1 teaspoon of French mustard and blend with the contents of the dish. Let the carrots steep in the liquid for at least a few hours before serving; even a day or two will not be too long.

Carrots à la Vichy

Vichy water, springing from the limefree soil of this famous resort, is good for people who have punished their livers. Carrots, too, are a famous health food. Carrots à la Vichy are certainly very wholesome.
Place the prepared carrots into a saucepan in which you have melted a good lump of butter. Add a pinch of salt, and enough water to cover the carrots – not Vichy water, although a pinch

How to grow roots

Root seeds must never be grown in recently manured soil, or the roots become fanged and forked. In a rotation plan roots do well in a plot which was used the year before for members of the cabbage family.

Carrot

Carrots need good soil and are sown every month from early spring to summer. Sow thinly, ½in (2cm) in fine tilth – no stones – in a warm, sunny place. Thin as soon as possible, and then again until the plants are 2–3in (5–8cm) apart, timing this operation so that the thinnings are large enough to be used in the kitchen in a mixture of vegetables, or eaten raw. Late main-crop carrots for storing are lifted, stripped of their greenery and packed in sand in a frost-proof place. They can also be stored in a clamp (piled in a pyramid, surrounded with straw and then covered with earth).

Beetroot

Sow seeds of the round variety in spring in rows 12in (30cm) apart and 1in (3cm) deep. Sow them thinly and thin out to 4in (10cm) apart. Sow again in late spring or early summer using the long varieties. A summer sowing will give you beetroots in winter. Lift them as required, or you could store them in boxes or clamps like carrots.

Swede

Hardy roots, they are sown in summer and thinned to 12in (30cm) apart. They can be left in the ground until wanted.

Turnip

Sow a few at a time in succession. Turnips, being related to the brassicas, make delicious green tops. For a plentiful supply of this greenery sow in late summer and do not thin out. Otherwise, turnips are thinned out to 6in (15cm) apart. There are round ones, long ones, pink and white and green varieties: all need lots of watering.

Celeriac

This delicious root with a strong celery flavour needs good, rich ground like stalk celery, to which it is closely related. However, it needs no earthing up and no fussing. Its seedlings are raised in boxes or pots filled with compost and, when they are large enough to handle, they are planted out, as firmly as possible without damaging the roots, in shallow drills 18in (45cm) apart with 10–12in (25–30cm) between the plants. It grows on the flat rather than being deeply buried. But for the trimming of any side shoots so that only the bulbous main stem matures, and a bit of watering and some hoeing between the rows and plants, it needs very little attention. In maturity, a celeriac may weigh up to 4lb (2kg), so a few will go quite a long way, and it hardly matters that the greenery, which appears in a thatch at the top of each head, is little use in the kitchen. Roots may be left in the ground until needed. Frost will not harm them, but in case of a hard winter it may be more convenient to store them in a shed.

of bicarbonate of soda added to tap-water will help you to get closer to the real thing. Put the lid on the pan and cook gently until all the liquid has evaporated. Shake the pan occasionally. If the carrots appear to stick to the bottom, add a little water spoonful by spoonful. This produces glistening carrot-coloured carrots.

Glazed carrots

In this dish the object is to produce rich, old-master-varnished carrots. 1lb (450g) of young carrots go into the pot with 1 heaped tablespoon of sugar, 4 tablespoons of butter, enough good brown stock to cover them, and a pinch of salt. Leave the lid off the pan. Boil briskly at first, then proceed exactly as for Vichy carrots. By the time the carrots are tender, the liquid will have reduced to a rich glaze. Carefully roll the carrots about in this, so that each one is nicely coated, and serve with a sprinkling of very finely chopped parsley.

French carrots

A la crème: simmer the carrots in so little water that it has completely evaporated by the time they are tender. Then add a small amount of butter and enough heated cream to cover them, and reduce by boiling until the sauce has reached the consistency of thick custard. This makes a good accompaniment to breast of veal, or any other dryish joint. *Au jus:* as above, but add veal stock instead of cream.

German carrots: add a walnut of butter and a sprinkling of flour. Blend until the vegetables are barely coated.

Casseroled carrots

This is a good main dish for lunch: 1 thick slice of bacon, some carrots and 2 onions are required. Cut the carrots into rectangular chunks and together with the chopped onions, put them in a casserole in which the bacon, cut in cubes, has been rendered and slightly browned. Cover closely and cook in a medium oven until they are tender. They will take about 1 hour. Then remove the lid, add a sprinkling of grated cheese, and brown the top. Serve with a plain salad or a fresh green vegetable.

Brandade of carrots

A smooth purée the consistency of mashed potatoes is traditionally made with salt cod; with carrots, and eaten with fried bread, it makes an attractive pale pink lunch dish.
Mince raw carrots. Do not liquidize them – you want a little texture. Place them in a saucepan with 1 crushed clove of garlic and just enough liquid (stock or water) to prevent burning. Stir constantly over gentle heat until cooked through, then add an equal quantity of a really stiff Béchamel sauce, and pile the purée on a dish.

Carrots and peas

This is one of the prettiest vegetable dishes. Add cooked carrots to a saucepan of freshly cooked green peas and heat them through, shaking the pan over the heat, so that the carrots and peas are evenly distributed. Dish up. The fresh reds and greens look cheerful enough without any sprinkling of parsley, but if you have a few asparagus tips or stalks cut into pea-sized pieces, these make a good addition. In Germany, where this is the traditional dish to herald the summer, it is usually crowned with a Morel.

Carrot cake (*makes a 9in (23cm) cake of 3 layers*)

8oz (225g; 2 cups) plain flour	$\frac{1}{2}$ pint ($\frac{1}{4}$l; 1 cup) corn oil
2 level teaspoons cinnamon	2 drops vanilla essence
pinch salt	4 eggs
2 level teaspoons baking powder	$1\frac{1}{4}$lb (560g) carrots, grated
15oz (425g; 2 cups) sugar	5oz (135g; $1\frac{1}{4}$ cups) walnuts, chopped

Preheat the oven to moderate (Reg 4/350°F). Butter and flour three 9in (23cm) cake or sponge tins. Sieve the flour, cinnamon, salt and baking powder together. Cream the sugar and oil together until they are a smooth creamy mixture. Add the vanilla, then the eggs one at a time, alternating with the sieved dry ingredients and the grated carrot. Add the nuts. Divide the mixture evenly between the 3 tins and bake for 45 minutes. Leave the layers in the tins for a few minutes before turning them out on to racks to cool. They are particularly soft, so they need very gentle handling.

Cream cheese icing

3oz (75g; $\frac{3}{8}$ cup) butter	3oz (75g; $\frac{3}{4}$ cup) walnuts, chopped
8oz (225g; 1 cup) best cream cheese	1 or 2 drops vanilla essence
8oz (225g; $1\frac{3}{4}$ cups) icing sugar	6 tablespoons cream, lightly whipped

Cream together the butter, cream cheese, icing sugar, nuts and vanilla essence. Fold in the whipped cream and spread the mixture between the layers and over the outside of the cake when it has cooled.

BEETROOT *Beta vulgaris*

'The Great and beautifull Beete' was introduced to Northern Europe at the end of the sixteenth century, by way of seeds brought from the Mediterranean regions. In his *Herbal*, Gerard highly praised it, as giving pleasure to the palate and the eye. Its 'perfect purple juyce tending to rednesse' supplied sought-after high colour in Renaissance meals, gradually displacing the powdered sandalwood (saunders) with which English cooks had hitherto added visual interest to their dishes. Both roots and leaves of the red beet had of course been used by the Ancients; and the Russians, whose most famous culinary achievement is *borscht*, the beautiful beetroot soup, use them still. Beetroot leaves, which are

Beetroot *Beta vulgaris*

cooked like spinach, are one of the most valuable sources of vitamin A and C, and also iron. The roots contain some vitamin A, B and C, and also calcium and iron; about 70 calories a helping.

Basic treatment

To boil beetroot to use cold later, trim the greenery, leaving longish stumps. Do not cut off the tapering root, for any nick in the skin will cause the beetroot to bleed when you put it in water. To boil, allow about 30 minutes for freshly harvested roots of medium size; old large beetroot may need as long as 2 hours. Beetroot that has been damaged is better baked in a slow oven, wrapped in buttered paper or foil; this will take from 30 minutes to 1½ hours, depending on size.

Jellied beetroot soup (*for 2*)

2 onions	peppercorns
4 carrots	1 lump sugar
4 beetroot	dash vinegar
½ lemon	1 teaspoon gelatine crystals
parsley	sour cream

Boil together in 1½ pints (1l; 3 cups) salted water all the vegetables, the parsley and the lemon with the peppercorns, until they are exhausted and have given all their flavour to the stock. Peel the cooked beetroot and grate them into a bowl. Strain the vegetable stock over them. Return the mixture to the pan (discard the vegetables other than the beetroot) and

heat through. Add the sugar and a dash of vinegar; do not let it boil. Strain after 10 minutes. Add the gelatine softened in 1 teaspoon of the hot soup, dissolve it thoroughly, and chill. Serve this delicate, beautifully coloured jelly with sour cream.

Russian borscht (*for 6*)

2lb (900g) raw beetroot	vinegar
1 white cabbage	salt
1 bunch thyme	pepper
5 pints (2¾l; 10 cups) stock	6 tablespoons sour cream or
1 tablespoon lard or butter	yoghourt

Peel the beetroot and cut all except 2 into small pieces. This soup depends on the beetroot yielding its colour. Cut three-quarters of the cabbage into slices and put the cut-up beet-root, the sliced cabbage and the thyme into the strained stock. Bring this to the boil and let it simmer for 1½ to 2 hours until the vegetables have lost their texture and colour. Strain the stock and return it to the pan.

Using a mandoline, slice the remaining quarter of the cabbage into thin little matchstick strips and grate the 2 uncooked beetroot coarsely. Fry the beetroot in lard for 1 or 2 minutes, sprinkle it with vinegar, and add it and the sliced cabbage to the strained claret-coloured stock. The beetroot will take 12 minutes to cook from this moment and will colour the stock a rich ruby-red. Season with salt and pepper, and serve with a spoonful of sour cream or yoghourt.

Clear sweet-sour borscht (*for 6*)

Preparation of this soup, which is made from fermented beetroot juice and stock, needs to be started 2 days before you intend to have it. Cut 2 raw beetroot into chunks, cover with lukewarm water, and float a piece of rye-bread on top. Place the bowl in a warm place. After 48 hours, fermentation will have taken place. Strain the liquid, season with salt, pepper and a pinch of sugar, and mix with an equal quantity of good clear stock. Serve with dollops of sour cream.

Thick beetroot soup

Cut up and bake a large beetroot in the oven. When it is quite soft, pass it through a sieve and mix the red purée with an equal quantity of mashed potatoes. (This is a very good way of using up left-over cooked potatoes, which never reheat satisfactorily on their own.) Dilute with stock, bring to the boil, stirring hard to keep the soup smooth, season, and at the last moment add some walnuts of butter and some chopped herbs. Chervil is the classic addition.

Beetroot and apple hash

Peel and cut up finely 2 cooked beetroot, and reheat them in a pan in which a chopped onion has been softened in butter, but not browned. Add a large, peeled and roughly chopped-up apple, and cook the mixture over the lowest heat until you have a coarse purée. If there is too much drying-out during the cooking process, add water in small quantities, and work in some extra butter. Season and eat with sausages, cold or hot roast pork, or on its own with sippets of fried bread.

Marjoram beetroot

6 medium beetroot	juice of ½ lemon
2 tablespoons butter	salt
marjoram	pepper

Boil the beetroot until tender, or bake in the oven. Melt the butter, and blend in ½ teaspoon marjoram and the lemon juice. Peel and slice or dice the beet and work in the butter mixture. Season, and serve with fried potatoes and ham or cold meat. Celeriac is good mixed in too. It should be boiled until soft but *al dente*, slightly crisper than the beetroot.

Beetroot haché on toast

Simmer some beetroot for 15 minutes in butter with parsley, crushed garlic, a dusting of flour, a little vinegar, salt and pepper. Mash and cool. Mix with thick cream, Worcestershire sauce and heap on toast.

Beetroot à la crème

Parboil the beetroot. Peel and cut it into neat round slices, or half circles if the vegetable is enormous. To finish the cooking process, stew the slices of beetroot in butter until they are soft, sprinkle with a few drops of lemon juice, and keep warm in a vegetable dish. Dilute the pan juices with a generous dash of thick cream, bring to the boil and simmer until thick. Season, and pour over the waiting beetroot. Instead of pure cream, Béchamel sauce, enriched with extra cream, can be more economically used. Eat with fried bread or, as a side dish, with pork or veal.

SWEDES *Brassica napobrassica*

Swedes contain some vitamin B and C. They are low in calories: about 30 in an average helping.

The outward appearance of this vegetable does not do it justice; it tastes a great deal better than it looks.

Treat a swede in the same way as you would a middle-aged turnip. In fact, all turnip recipes can be applied to swedes. Large ones are very good boiled and mashed with butter and a pinch of nutmeg, or used in soups. Swedes should be thickly peeled and diced for boiling, and any left-over purée can be mixed with mashed potato for topping shepherd's pie. Swedes, like parsnips, are excellent when roasted. Cut them into strips, parboil them for about 5 minutes, then arrange them round the meat to roast for about 1 hour. They become crisp and golden; nicer than potatoes.

TURNIP *Brassica napus*

The then Secretary of State Lord Townshend revolutionized eighteenth-century British agriculture by putting fields under turnips during the periods in which they traditionally lay fallow. The British took years to realize that turnips were a valuable source of nourishment for man and beast, but George I, newly arrived from his native Hanover to ascend the throne of England, Ireland and Scotland (where even the swede is called turnip), was deeply impressed. He went so far as to ask how much it would cost to plough up St James's Park for extra space in which to grow them. 'Turnip' Townshend replied: 'Only three crowns, Sir.' St James's remained a romantically landscaped park, and turnips did not become a cause of national outcry, although to say that they have ever become popular would be claiming too much. They may not be the most attractive vegetables in the world, but when they are *small* – no larger than an overgrown radish – they make very good eating.

High in essential mineral content and low in vitamins, boiled turnips have a surprisingly low calorie content for a member of the root family. An average helping, without sauce, yields only about 40 calories.

Basic treatment

Scrub, trim and skin (*see* Carrots) when young. Peel and cut into cubes when old. Depending on age, they take up to 30 minutes boiling time.

Boiled turnips

Turnips are all the better for being boiled in a good stock:

18

chicken or bacon stock, for example. They should be well seasoned with salt and freshly ground black pepper. They can be served with butter, mashed into a purée with thick cream, or served with a Béchamel sauce mixed with a little mustard.

Turnip soup (*for 4*)

1½lb (675g) turnips	5 slices bread
2 onions	2 egg yolks
2oz (50g; ¼ cup) butter	seasoning
2 pints (1¼l; 4 cups) water	large dash of cream

Coarsely chop the peeled turnips and skinned onions, and soften them over gentle heat in the butter. Add the water, and boil up briskly. Add the bread after cutting off the crusts, and simmer for 20 minutes. When all is tender, sieve or liquidize. Reheat, stirring in the egg yolks, which you have beaten separately in a little of the soup, until they emulsify. Take care that the soup remains below boiling point. Season. Add the cream, not so much stirring it in as dragging it over the surface.

French turnip soup (*for 4–5*)

6 young turnips	2 pints (1¼l; 4 cups)
3 medium-sized potatoes	vegetable stock
1 small onion	salt
1 small leek	pepper
2oz (50g; ¼ cup) butter	2 small egg yolks
1oz (25g; ¼ cup) flour	4 tablespoons thick cream

Scrape the turnips and dice them, peel and chop the potatoes and the onion, and roughly chop the leek. Cook all the vegetables in the butter over a gentle heat for about 10 minutes, but do not let them brown. Remove the pan from the heat and stir in the flour. Return the pan to the stove and cook the mixture for a few minutes, stirring constantly. Add the stock gradually, and season with salt and pepper. Cover the pan, and simmer gently until the vegetables are well cooked and collapsed. You can then put the mixture through the coarse blade of a mouli, but soup is more satisfying when it is full of interesting bits and pieces of vegetable. Beat the egg yolks into the cream in a separate basin and pour in a little of the hot soup. Mix well and return to the pan. Heat through gently, and serve with parsley.

Caramelized turnips

Small young turnips should be cooked very quickly. Scrape and chop them into walnut-sized pieces, blanch them for about 5 minutes in boiling salted water, and then drain. Melt a good lump of butter in a heavy shallow pan, and fry the turnips over a high flame with a sprinkling of sugar, keep them on the move with a wooden spoon. They should emerge brown and glossy. Sprinkle on more sugar to caramelize if they are not browning; delicious with duck.

Turnips with breadcrumbs and parsley

Scrape 2lb (900g) of tiny turnips and cook them for 10 minutes in boiling salted water. Drain them, cut them in halves and fry them in olive oil for about 15 minutes or until the turnips are tender. Add a good handful of breadcrumbs mixed with chopped onion and chopped parsley, and shake the pan over the heat until the breadcrumbs have soaked up all the olive oil and have turned crisp and golden; delicious eaten with large cuts of meat such as rib-roasts.

Indian turnips (*for 4–6*)

1½lb (675g) tiny young turnips	1 tablespoon poppy seed
4 tablespoons clarified butter	¼ teaspoon ginger
½lb (225g) chopped onions	¼ teaspoon cayenne
4 tablespoons cream	1 teaspoon turmeric
6 tablespoons yoghourt	½ teaspoon cummin
water to moisten	1 tablespoon ground coriander
aromatics:	6 cloves garlic infused in a little boiling water
2 tablespoons ground sesame seed	2 tablespoons parsley, chopped

Scrape the turnips and prick them all over with a fork. Fry them in a bit of the butter until they look crisp on the outside, then put them to one side. In the rest of the butter, fry the onions with the sesame, poppy seed, ginger, cayenne and turmeric, stirring well. Moisten with a few spoonfuls of water and simmer until dry. Add 4 tablespoons water, and simmer until dry again. Add the turnips, cummin and coriander, and cook for 5 minutes. Add the salt, the garlic infusion, and half the yoghourt, and once more cook until dry. Add the remaining yoghourt, and when that too has finally evaporated, mix in the cream and the parsley. Transfer the mixture into a fireproof dish and bake in a medium oven for 15 minutes.

Turnip tops

The stalks of old turnips that have gone to seed can be peeled, tied in bundles, cooked like asparagus in plenty of boiling salted water, and eaten with melted butter.

CELERIAC *Apium graveolens rapaceum*

This turnip-shaped vegetable – about 30 calories a helping – which eighteenth-century cookbooks refer to as a native of Sardinia is a close relation of celery, but esteemed for its base alone. The stems are not much use in the kitchen.

Basic treatment

Peel the celeriac – the skin is tough, but a really sharp cook's knife is half the battle – then quarter or cut into chunks or slices. Some dishes require strips as thin as matchsticks. Celeriac can also be eaten raw, but then it must be grated. Boiling time, from 20–30 minutes.

SHOOTS/STALKS

Celery *Apium graveolens*

Celery was cultivated by the Romans from a wild plant which is known as smallage in the English countryside. Long after the Roman empire had crumbled, however, celery was still known as 'Italian food . . . the young shoots thereof eat raw with oyl and pepper.' Celery tea was recommended to sufferers from gout and rheumatism, while bathing toes and fingers in a hot strong decoction was said to ease the chilblains that inevitably appeared during the frosty northern winters.

CELERY *Apium graveolens*

A slimmer's standby, celery has a negligible calorie content, traces of vitamin B and C and some inorganic minerals.

Basic treatment

Wipe clean; trim discoloured edges of outer stalks. Separate the stalks, pulling from the base to remove the stringy fibres.

Discard the leaves (except when you serve celery with cheese, when you need them for prettiness). Celery is cut differently for different uses. For salads, cut across the stalk into $\frac{1}{4}$in (1cm) pieces. For use as a flavouring agent in soups and stews, cut into about 2in (5cm) chunks. For braised celery, cut across the plant about 3in (8cm) from the base, which should also be neatly trimmed (keep the stalks for other purposes). If the celery is enormous, halve the heads by a vertical cut.
Boiling: 10–20 minutes will soften celery, but the longer it is left to cook, the more of its flavour is imparted to the dish.
Braising: blanch the celery for 5 minutes, drain and cook for about 30 minutes in a covered casserole.

How to grow celery
Celery needs very rich ground (plenty of compost at the bottom of the trench). Sow in late spring in seed compost; seeds need heat to germinate. Prick off little seedlings into boxes of compost, keep them growing steadily, but not overwatered, and plant out in summer. Plants should be 6–9in (15–23cm) apart. When they are 10–12in (25–30cm) high, plants may be given a paper collar held with paper clips, and earthed up to blanch. Earthing up is done two or three times, but never above the base of the leaves.

1. Celery is planted into trenches which are gradually filled up

2. Careful earthing up keeps the stalks white

Thick celery soup

In a large pan, assemble the carcass, feet and giblets of a chicken, 1 onion, 1 carrot, 1 bayleaf and 1 large head of celery. Cover with cold water, bring to the boil, and allow to simmer for at least 30 minutes, then strain. Allow 1 egg yolk for each $\frac{1}{2}$ pint ($\frac{1}{4}$l; 1 cup) of liquid. In a basin beat the egg yolks well with a drop or two of lemon juice. Pour some of the broth into the eggs, whisking all the time to ensure that they are well combined before returning the mixture to the remaining broth. Stir the soup over a low heat until hot and thick, but on no account let it boil. Season with salt and pepper, and serve with a sprinkling of chopped parsley and a swirl of thick cream.

This recipe can be adapted for celeriac.

Waldorf salad (*for 4*)

This is a very good fresh winter salad and surprisingly very filling (probably because of all the chewing you have to do).

It is also a good way of eating cold roast turkey.

1 head crisp celery	4 thick slices cold roast
4 nice firm apples	turkey or chicken
juice of $\frac{1}{2}$ lemon	olive oil
1 handful shelled walnuts	1 egg yolk
salt, pepper	1 heart of lettuce

Cut the celery sticks into little crescents. Peel, quarter and core the apples and cut them into cubes. Put them in a bowl and squeeze lemon juice all over them. Add the halved shelled walnuts and the chicken or turkey cut into cubes, and season them with salt and pepper. Add a few tablespoons of olive oil and 1 egg yolk, and stir it all round so that everything is well covered. Just before serving the salad, arrange the best inner leaves of the lettuce around the sides of the bowl. Taste to see if the dressing is sharp enough, and if necessary, add more lemon juice.

Céleri rémoulade

Blanch matchstick pieces of celeriac for 3 minutes in briskly boiling salted water acidulated with a dash of vinegar. Drain and dry well in a cloth. Then mix in a mayonnaise made with plenty of Dijon mustard. This is the high spot of that great standby, the *crudités*, consisting of, say, grated raw carrots, shredded raw cabbage, thinly sliced cucumbers, baby radishes left whole, and whatever other raw vegetable is to hand – the point being that all the different ingredients are separately dressed and served in separate dishes at the same time. *Céleri rémoulade*, however, is so good that it makes a splendid first course on its own.

Celeriac salad

Blend a diced head of cooked celeriac with a few diced cooked potatoes, and a small diced cooked beetroot in a good mayonnaise: this will turn mauvey pink. Just before serving, add some sliced raw chicory for crunchiness, and some julienne strips of apple. The salad goes wonderfully well with left-over poultry, particularly turkey.

Celery, orange and onion salad (*for 6*)

2 large oranges	wine vinegar
1 medium-sized onion	olive oil
2 heads celery	salt, pepper

Peel the oranges as if they were apples, making a continuous spiral of peel. You need a very sharp small knife and you must cut right through, removing all the pith and leaving the orange bare and glistening. Slice the oranges on a plate, keeping all the juice, and put it in a bowl. Peel the onion and slice it as thinly as possible; clean and cut the celery into $\frac{1}{4}$in (1cm) crescents. Add these to the salad. Make a dressing using the orange juice with a little wine vinegar, olive oil, salt, pepper, but no garlic. Stir in, and leave in a cool place or in a refrigerator before serving.

Pigeons in celery sauce (*for 4*)

2 heads celery	glass red wine
2 onions	a little salt
1in (3cm) thick slice	plenty of pepper
streaky bacon in a piece	1 tablespoon flour worked
butter	into 1 tablespoon butter
1 young pigeon per person	*beurre manié*
dusting of flour	3 or 4 tablespoons cream

Cut the celery into ½in (1cm) pieces, coarsely chop the onions, and dice the bacon. Heat the butter in a fireproof casserole, and add the bacon. When it sizzles, brown the pigeons, dusted all over with flour. Remove them to a plate and sweat the vegetables in the casserole, covered, for a few minutes. Lay the pigeons on top and pour the wine over everything. Season, cover, and simmer on top of the stove or in the oven for about 1½ hours, or until the pigeons are tender. Put the pigeons on a hot dish and keep them warm, together with the vegetables. Skim most of the fat off the juice and thicken with *beurre manié*. The juice is copious, most of it coming from the celery. Taste for seasoning, and stir in the cream. Pour the sauce over the birds and the vegetables, and serve with potato purée.

Celery au gratin (*for 6 when served as a first course; 3 when it is the main dish*)

3 heads celery	3oz (75g; ¾ cup) cheese
1 lump butter	salt, pepper
2 tablespoons flour	thick cream
½ pint (¼l; 1 cup) milk	breadcrumbs

Keeping the heads of celery whole, drop them into a large pan of boiling salted water, and let them cook for about 20 minutes. Meanwhile, make a cheese sauce with the butter, flour, milk, grated cheese and seasoning.

Drain the celery, cut the heads in half and lay them, cut side down, in a gratin dish. Pour over the sauce, and then the cream. Sprinkle with breadcrumbs, dot with butter, and bake for 20 minutes in a fairly hot oven (Reg 6/400°F). If this is to be a main dish, you can make it more nourishing by rolling up the celery heads in slices of cooked ham before pouring on the cheese sauce.

Celery to go with game

Celery, first blanched, sprinkled with lemon juice, and then very gently stewed with as much butter as you can spare, makes a nice vegetable to go with hare, or venison.

CHICORY *Cichorium intybus*

This tightly rolled parcel of fleshy leaves, known as endive in the USA and in France, used to be grown under the name of succory in medieval cottage gardens. It was highly esteemed for its summer greenery. The fact that the roots, when lifted and forced into a second growth in the dark yielded white fleshy shoots (called *chicons*) more succulent and less bitter than the first crop of leaves, was discovered by chance, and confusion about the name has reigned ever since.

Its ancestor is called *Cichorium endivia*, which grows in many varieties, from Batavian endive to the curly-mopped green head which is known as endive in England, *chicorée* in France and chicory in the USA (see page 61). From time immemorial this has been used as a salad plant and a pot vegetable in spite of its bitter tang. Perhaps its very bitterness made our ancestors regard it as a medicinal plant, 'refreshing to the weake and fainting spirit' when eaten raw, and 'like to encrease the bloud if sodd in white broth.'

However, even then it was described as being 'more tender and delicate for being whited', which was achieved by putting a slate or a plate over the growing plant. But it is with the succulent variety, *Cichorium intybus*, with its ivory-tinged leaves, that cooks are now mostly concerned.

How to grow chicory

The most common kind grown is the Brussels chicory which produces white shoots or chicons for winter salads. There is also a very pretty red variety called Red Verona. The seeds are sown in well-cultivated soil in late spring–early summer and thinned out three weeks later to 8in (20cm) apart. A pretty green plant will develop through the summer, and when the leaves begin to die down in the autumn the roots, which are like parsnips, should be lifted. It is a good idea to leave them on the surface of the soil for a few days to retard the growth. The foliage is cut off and the pointed end of the root, leaving a thick root about 8in (20cm) long and 2in (5cm) across at the thick end. These roots are then stored in sand or soil in a cool place. For forcing put the roots, 5 or 6 upright in a large pot, or more in a bucket or box, and pack sand, soil or peat round them and about 3in (8cm) deep over them. In a week or two the white, pointed, solid chicons will appear for your winter salads. The taste is pleasantly sharp and fresh. The red types are produced in the same way.

Basic treatment

Raw chicory is very low in calories, only about 35 in 1lb (450g). Wipe well, and trim off any damaged outer leaves. Chicory discolours easily, so cut it, if cutting is required, directly before using it. Its characteristic bitterness can be reduced by blanching it; 3 minutes in boiling water is sufficient, but this, of course, works only in cooked chicory dishes.

Red, white and green salad

This dish, with its patriotic Italian colour scheme, is made by mixing chicory, cut into chunks, with green beans and strips of sweet red peppers in a French dressing. The white of the chicory should predominate.

Chicory and egg sauce

This sauce, which goes well with poultry or any white meat, calls for boiled chicory, which is usually to be deplored, but not in this case; what you are making is a smooth sauce with an interesting taste. Prepare 4 white heads of chicory by blanching and chopping them into small pieces. Cook them in salted water until they are very soft. Drain and rinse them under the cold tap in a colander. Press out the excess liquid. Make a little white roux, using 1 tablespoon of flour. Draw of the heat, add 2 egg yolks beaten with the top of the milk, a few drops of lemon juice, and the chicory. Season. Place the pan in a *bain-marie* and cook the sauce until it has thickened to the consistency of custard. Serve at once.

Creamy chicory salad

Mix 2 large sliced heads of chicory with a handful of currants, soaked to plump them, 1 large diced apple, and a few blanched chopped almonds. For the dressing, mix together 6 tablespoons of mayonnaise and 3 tablespoons of whipped cream. Fold in the dry ingredients, chill well and serve with cold ham or any other cold meat.

Caramelized chicory in butter

Heat over a gentle flame 4oz (100g) of butter in a fireproof casserole with a tightly fitting lid. Place the trimmed heads of chicory in the golden liquid, add a pinch of salt, a small teaspoon of sugar, and a good squeeze of lemon juice. Reduce the heat, cover, and cook for a few minutes until the vegetables have rendered some of their own juice. Then raise the flame, and cook for about 15 minutes until they are tender and the sugar has caramelized.

FENNEL *Foeniculum vulgare*

What a fourteenth-century writer calls 'the vertuous Fennel' fully deserves its epithet, for there is no confusion about it. The name remains the same although there are two main varieties: the vegetable or Italian fennel with a bulbous enlargement at the base of the stalks, used for cooking; and the green and bronze fennels that support their feathery fronds on slender stems, used more for flavouring. The properties with which this vegetable, regardless of variety, is credited, are truly remarkable. It was thought 'to asswage the wamblings of the Stomache', to engender sleep and, conversely, to sharpen both sight and brain. It was recommended to seventeenth-century weight-watchers; those who had grown fat were exhorted to drink fennel broth much and often 'to abate their unwieldinesse and make them more gaunt and lank.' *Finocchio* or Florence fennel is grown mostly like celery; it contains much the same nutrients, and is, of course, distinct from its relative, the feathery herb. The leaves of Florence or sweet fennel – small bright green plumes tasting of aniseed – can also be chopped up and used as flavouring,

but the charm of the plant lies in its bulbous ribbed bases the size of a duck's egg. These need a good warm summer in which to form, and are good eaten raw, in salad; classic with fish; delicious braised; not worth eating boiled. All celery recipes apply to fennel.

SEAKALE *Crambe maritima*

This contains vitamin C and very few calories. It is eaten like asparagus, and needs plenty of butter. The vegetable still grows wild on the coasts in great rosettes of stalks which end in crinkly crests. As it creeps under the shingle it is naturally blanched. Its delicate, slightly nutty flavour recommended itself to French gourmets: it was cultivated by the royal gardeners in France in the early nineteenth century. It is all too rarely grown in our vegetable gardens.

Plants are put in and well fed in spring. In mid-winter they are covered with leaves or black polythene to produce plump shoots. Start cutting the plants when they are young.

Basic treatment

Wash the stalks, cut off the leaves. Tie the seakale in bundles, and cook until tender (15–20 minutes); steaming it will take about 35 minutes and will preserve the flavour better. Serve with any of the sauces you would use with asparagus.

The leaves make a delicious salad; put plenty of herbs into the dressing.

BEAN SPROUTS *Phaseolus mungo*

Special beans to produce the authentic shoots that are used with such effect in oriental cooking can be bought from all enterprising seedsmen. You grow them not in the open but in the warmth of the kitchen; and not in soil but on a tray lined with moistened cottonwool or well-dampened newspapers. Soak the washed beans overnight, and in the morning distribute them evenly over their damp base. Slip the tray into a large polythene bag to preserve the moisture, and cover with brown paper to exclude the light. The bean sprouts will take 6 to 9 days to be ready for eating. They should be about 1–1½in (2·5–3·5cm) to be at their best.

Basic treatment

Remove the bean-hulls, and wash the shoots. Blanch them for 2 minutes in boiling salted water, not longer, for crispness is their great asset. Drain and eat them with butter and a sprinkling of soya sauce. Bean sprouts contain vitamins B, C and E. One helping yields less than 25 calories.

Bean shoots are a good addition to dishes of diced mixed vegetables. For a chop suey you would cover the vegetable mixture with a thin egg-blanket, made with eggs that are well-beaten to fluidity, allowed to spread over the bottom of a greased pan, and set rather than fried. They should retain their colour and not be in the least browned.

BULBS

Bulbs of the onion family – onions, leeks, garlic – were already known and cultivated by the Ancient World. The ancient Egyptians held onions sacred. 'To bite into one,' said the Roman writer Juvenal, 'would have been sacrilege. Oh blessed nation, to see their gods growing in their gardens.' The onion, prized for its flavour, was enjoyed by the Romans and Greeks alike. They ate it raw, with a little salt, for breakfast, and it became an essential ingredient in countless prepared dishes. Oddly, considering its pungency, it was also regarded as an aphrodisiac, and a symbol of fertility.

ONION *Allium cepa*

Calories: 7 per ounce; the protein, iron and carbohydrate content is low; there is little calcium, no fat.

There are many varieties of onion on the market. Seedsmen describe the gradations of flavour in terms of mild, sweet, warm and good. As a rule of thumb, the larger they are, the blander.

It is easy to cultivate onions from seed or from sets. These pre-grown bulblets can grow into gigantic globes, the circumference of a saucer – unless the pigeons, who are all too fond of them, pull them before they mature. Seedsmen recommend them because there is no thinning out to be done in the rows, but the pleasure of seeing green eyelashes emerging from the drills is too great to forgo this altogether, and one must cater for the enjoyment of pulling your own spring onion – seedlings, to be eaten in salads, or with cheese, or by themselves with salt, crusty bread and butter.

Sometimes onions should be used unpeeled, especially in soups, which will assume a delicately bright gold if onion peel is added to the pot; fish it out before serving – an easy exercise as it will float at the top. (Onion skins are also splendid for dyeing Easter eggs yellow – anything from primrose

Onion
Allium cepa

to daffodil, depending on how long the eggs are boiled in the dye.)

However, most dishes require their onions skinned. As the bulbs contain a strong and acrid essence which makes your tear ducts work overtime, onion peeling is a weepy business. One remedy that appears to work is to clamp a piece of bread between the teeth during peeling and chopping. You may look idiotic during the operation, but you will emerge dry-eyed; a waste of bread, perhaps, but a saving of handkerchiefs. Or peel them under running cold water, or hold a matchstick between your teeth – these methods are also said to work.

Many dishes would not be as delicious as they are if it were not for the use of onions. Cooking *à la lyonnaise*, or *à la bourguignonne*, means onions, sliced and lightly fried or

tiny silver onions left whole. It is the agreeable slipperiness of onions that makes them ideal accompaniments for drier kinds of meat like breast of veal, or liver, or even mealy vegetables like green peas past their prime.

Basic treatment

Onions are among the very few garden vegetables that are better in maturity than in their first youth. It is true that spring onions taste marginally sweeter when they are freshly pulled, but for all cooking purposes, onions are better used fully grown, when they have a papery, toast-coloured skin.

Peel this skin away, and trim the roots. To boil onions, put them into salted water from 10–30 minutes, depending on size and freshness. To braise, parboil, scoop out and bake, again depending on size and density of stuffing, from 30 minutes to 1 hour. For shallow-frying, slice and put them into a pan in which fat has melted over gentle heat, and depending on the dish in preparation, draw off the flame when they are anything from transparent to golden.

How to grow onions

For onion sets, sow in winter under glass; for especially large onions, sow in late summer or autumn. Transplant in late spring, screwing them into the ground 6in (15cm) apart. Replace any which are pulled up by the birds. Main sowing: late spring on light soil which has been well dug and manured in the winter and raked to a tilth. Regularly hoe between rows, and hand-weed the rows. Begin thinning when shoots are about 2in (5cm) high. Continue at intervals, until onions are 6in (15cm) apart. In summer, turn down the leaves to hasten ripening. When an onion is doing well it lifts itself up. Harvest and dry onions in the sun on a flat surface, turning them occasionally.

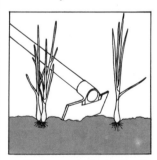

1. Hoe between drills; handweed rows. Thin to 4in (10cm) apart

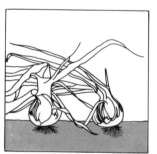

2. Bend the leaves in summer to hasten ripening

3. Harvest when onions sit on the ground

4. Make skeins; store in a dry airy place

Rich onion soup (*for 4 as a whole lunch or supper, for 6 as soup followed by something else – it is extremely filling*)

1lb (450g) onions	salt
2oz (50g; $\frac{1}{4}$ cup) butter	pepper
2 pints ($1\frac{1}{4}$l; 4 cups) good beef stock	1 teaspoon sugar
	1 French loaf
2 twigs or branches fennel	Gruyère cheese, grated
1 clove	brandy

Slice the onions, which should be the very large, round, mild ones, and soften them gently in the butter until they are transparent and bronzed. Bring the stock, as good and rich as it can be and if possible improved with some beef gravy, to the boil and pour it over the onions. Add the fennel, clove and seasoning. In a long-handled spoon hold a teaspoon of sugar under the heat until it caramelizes and turns deep brown. Add this to the soup – it will melt and give a mellow colour.

Simmer for 30 minutes and meanwhile toast slices of French bread and heap them with grated cheese, placing them in the bowls. Add a dash of brandy to the soup and ladle it over the bread. Sprinkle with more grated cheese, and stick the bowls under a very hot flame for a minute or two, until the surface is bubbling. Serve piping hot.

French onion soup (*for 6*)

This dish used to be the break-of-day refreshment for porters and sightseers at Les Halles *in Paris. The great central market halls have now gone, but the soup is still reviving and warming.*
Peel and slice about $1\frac{1}{2}$lb (675g) fist-sized onions. Melt a knob of butter in a large pan, and over gentle heat cook the onions until they are transparent and golden. Add about 3 pints ($1\frac{1}{2}$l; 6 cups) of liquid – pale stock is more nourishing but water will do, because the taste of the onions would mask any other flavour anyway. Season, and simmer for 30 minutes.

Thicken with 1½ tablespoons of flour blended in a little water, and continue simmering until the soup has thickened slightly. Draw off the flame and keep hot. Toast 6 thick slices of French bread, butter them, heap them generously with grated cheese, and put under the heat until the cheese has melted. Gruyère will produce the authentic long cheesy strands when the soup is spooned out, and is therefore best; but other sorts of hard yellow cheese will do at a pinch. Put these toasted cheese sandwiches into individual bowls, pour the hot soup over them, and add at least another tablespoon of grated cheese.

Mulligatawny soup (*for 6–8*)

This cold soup for hot days is not strictly an onion soup, but it would not be authentic without this useful bulb.

2 large onions	¼ pint (½ cup) single
2 pints (1¼l; 4 cups) chicken	cream
stock	1 cucumber
2 tablespoons curry powder	¼ pint (½ cup) thick cream

Slice the onions and put them in a saucepan with the chicken stock. Add the curry powder and simmer for 30 minutes. Remove the onions and add the single cream. Chill in the fridge. Peel the cucumber and cut into matchstick pieces. Chill. When the soup is iced, stir in the cucumber and the double cream, and serve with poppadums if you can get them. If you want to drink it hot, add some rice with the onion.

Onion and potato supper dish (*for 4*)

Take 2 large bunches of spring onions, trimmed and cut into short ½in (about 1cm) lengths right up to the green tips, and simmer in enough milk to cover. Boil 1lb (450g) of floury old potatoes, drain and mash. Add the onion-flavoured milk gradually, beating hard to make the purée as fluffy as possible. Season and pile in a dish and sprinkle with minutely chopped green ends of uncooked spring onion. Make a platform at the peak, pressing into it as much butter as you can spare. It will run down the side in rivulets, and continue doing so as you go on serving. A crisp green salad goes well with this.

Onion omelettes

Beat your eggs, and add very finely chopped spring onions – both white and green parts – to the mixture, as though you were making an *omelette aux fines herbes*. Make the omelette in the ordinary way, and serve with tomatoes and a plain French dressing.

Prepare a *purée soubise*: first blanch the onions, then melt them in butter to the transparent stage. Simmer them in a small amount of consommé or water, rub through a sieve, and blend with Béchamel sauce. When this mixture has been reduced over medium heat until it is stiff, make the omelette and fold in the purée.

For a medieval dish called hanoney (which is not strictly an omelette, but more like scrambled egg) brown some onions in a shallow pan, and pour the egg mixture over them at the last minute. Draw it about with a fork until set but not dry.

Stuffed onions

Large handsome onions farci *with a variety of stuffings make a good filling main course for lunch or dinner.*

For the stuffing you can use sausage meat, or any left-over cooked white meat (chopped fine, moistened with gravy and combined with a few fresh breadcrumbs), or a mixture of chopped mushrooms and a little ham or fresh minced beef bound with egg; almost any of the classic stuffings can be used and still leave plenty of room for experiment.

Choose a large handsome onion globe for each person. Peel, trim and scoop out part of the centre. Parboil the globes for 7 minutes in salted water. Drain upside down. Finely chop the centres which you have scooped out. Soften them in a shallow pan, and mix them with whatever stuffing you are using. Spoon the mixture into the drained onions, being careful not to press too hard or the globes will lose their shape. Place them in a casserole or stew-pan, add enough stock to come halfway up the onions, and cook hermetically sealed for about 1 hour. Check every now and then that the moisture has not evaporated. If the dish looks dry, add more liquid.

Crisp onion rings

Slice a large, skinned onion thickly and divide the slices into rings. Dip them first in milk, then in flour seasoned with salt and pepper. Plunge them into deep hot fat for about 3 minutes. Drain on crumpled kitchen paper, and serve with grilled or fried chops or steaks.

Onion au jus – *to go with roast beef or veal*

Trim and parboil 1½lb (675g) or so of little round onions. Drain and place in a pan with a slice of previously rendered fat bacon, 2 cloves, a bouquet of herbs, 1 lump of sugar and about 1 pint (¾l; 2 cups) of stock or water. Simmer for 1 hour, strain, put the onions aside and reduce the liquor by boiling it fast in an uncovered pan. Then replace the onions in the *jus* for as much time as it takes to reheat them. Serve with the joint.

Onions baked in the oven

This dish goes beautifully with veal, and is even nicer than onions cooked with the roast which never seems to have quite enough juice to prevent them from wrinkling up. Parboil as many large peeled onions as there are diners. Drain and place in a single layer in a fireproof dish with a sprinkling of seasoned flour. Then add some brown stock (which could be made with a soup cube) until the onions sit waist-high in the liquid. Basting frequently, bake the onions until they are tender. Before serving, mix a dash of thick cream with the liquor the onions were cooked in.

Stewed onions

If you do not have the oven going, but are planning onion globes as the accompaniment to sausages or any other dish which is not very juicy, this way of cooking them approximates to the baked onions in the previous recipe.

Allow as many large onions as there are people to feed. Top and tail, removing the papery skin, but taking care not to nick the onions themselves. Fry the onions lightly in butter, turning them this way and that so that they are nicely coated with fat all over. The put them side by side in a saucepan, barely cover with stock, and let them simmer for 1 hour or so. Season and serve.

Cream of onion soup (*for 4*)

Cut up 1lb (450g) onions, and let them soften but not colour in 2 tablespoons of melted but unbrowned butter over a low flame. Stir often, and sprinkle with 2 tablespoons of flour, stirring until you have an oniony roux. Gradually pour 1 pint (½l) water into the pan, allowing the mixture to come to the boil between additions, to prevent lumps forming. When all the liquid is absorbed, allow to simmer until the onions are quite soft. Finally replace the evaporated liquid in as much milk as is needed to make the soup thick and creamy. To gild the lily, you might like to add an egg yolk, beaten in a little milk; but then the soup must on no account be allowed to boil again.

Sage and onion stuffing – *for pork*

Bake 2 large unskinned onions in the oven until they are soft and squashy. Mince them – a fork should be all you need – and mix with enough white breadcrumbs to give you the consistency you like. For a very fluffy stuffing, beat in 1 whole egg. Then add 2 walnuts of butter, 2 tablespoons of chopped sage, season, and stuff the joint in the usual way. If you mean to cook the stuffing separately, bake it in a fireproof dish, having dotted the surface liberally with butter; or, form it into egg-sized individual portions and place these in the roasting tin 20 minutes before the meat is done.

Glazed onions – *as a garnish*

Trim and peel some tiny onions and toss them about in a little heated butter. Dust them with castor or icing sugar, and continue gently shaking the pan over low heat. Add enough water to barely cover them, and let them simmer, still shaking them occasionally; spoon liquid over them. When the moisture has practically evaporated, and you are left with a sticky glaze, roll the little onions about in this so that they are evenly coated. Arrange in little mounds or in a ring round a joint of meat.

Spring onions in French dressing

Tie spring onions trimmed to even lengths in a bunch, and cook until tender in salted water. Leave the pan uncovered so that the colour is not spoiled. Drain and cover with a

Vinaigrette sauce while hot. Serve either hot ot cold as part of an hors d'oeuvre that might consist of black olives, slices of salami and sliced, skinned tomatoes, all in separate dishes.

Bonfire onions

Bonfire picnics call for baked onions along with baked jacket potatoes and sausages. Wrap unpeeled, trimmed onions in buttered foil. Place them in a tin which should not be too shallow (an old biscuit tin would be ideal), and push this near the heart of the fire, covering the onions with hot ashes. After 1 hour or so, they will be tender and ready to eat by spooning out the centres.

LEEK *Allium porrum*

Leeks contain vitamins A, B and C and some inorganic mineral substances. They are in the medium group of calories – about 40 to a helping.

The old English word *leac* simply means plant. The first kitchen gardens were called 'leek gardens', and the early gardeners were 'leek wardens'. Leeks grew profusely all over the temperate zone. 'Friendly' is the adjective most used in connection with this vegetable, sometimes called 'the asparagus of the poor'. 'Friendly to stomach and liver', said a Dr Muffet in the middle of the seventeenth century; friendly, too, to the lungs, said Evelyn; and friendly, apparently, to the vocal chords, because Roman orators who valued the sonority of their voices beyond all else made a point of eating a great deal of it. Nero, who not only fiddled but sang his own compositions while Rome burned, is said to have enjoyed a daily helping of friendly leek soup. The Welsh chose the leek as their national emblem. This originated in the sixth century when the Celts were either playing some team game or making real war (opinions differ) against the Saxons. The Celtic leader, St David no less, ordered his men to wear leeks in their hats so that he might distinguish them from their opponents. The Celts won.

Basic treatment

Cut off the beard and any jagged wilting leaves. Wash carefully because the earth works itself in between the tightly packaged layers. Cut into rings or chunks, or leave whole, according to the dish you are preparing. If only the white part is required, save the greenery for flavouring stock, or use some of it, finely chopped, as you would a herb. Old leeks may take as long as 15 minutes to cook; young ones, freshly picked, may take less than 5 minutes, and it is the greatest pity to overcook them. Leeks are indispensable in the stockpot, where they can simmer just as long as the other ingredients; the longer they cook, the more their flavour is yielded, but unlike the roots, they will cease to be vegetables in their own right. Very old pungent leeks are sometimes blanched before the cooking process begins, but with leeks from the garden, even aged ones, this is never really necessary.

How to grow leeks

Leeks like well-enriched soil, so compost or manure in winter, and deep digging will keep them happy. The seeds are sown from very early to late spring in a seed bed and the young leeklets lifted with a fork when they are 6–8in (15–20cm) tall and planted into rows 9in (23cm) apart in drills. For planting, make holes 6in (15cm) deep in the bed with a small fork or a pencil. Drop the seedlings into the cavity and water, carrying the soil round the roots. Water well in dry weather, and draw earth gently up to the plants just before they are fully grown; this will keep them white. If you let a few plants run to seed, the flowerheads are useful for decoration.

1. Sow in a seed bed with plenty of space between the seeds

2. Lift at 6–8in (15–20cm)

3. Make holes, drop the seedlings in and water the soil down

4. Earth up slightly to keep leeks white

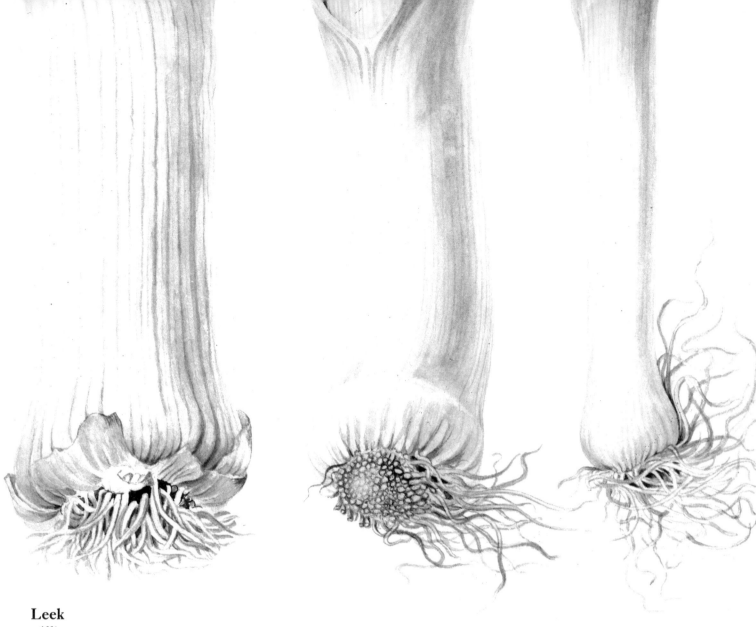

Leek
Allium porrum

Leek and onion soup (*for 4 as a main dish*)

1lb (450g) leeks	1 glass white wine
1lb (450g) onions	salt
2oz (50g; $\frac{1}{4}$ cup) butter	pepper
2 tablespoons flour	1 small carton single cream
$1\frac{1}{2}$ pints (1l; 3 cups) chicken stock	1 thick slice streaky bacon

Chop the cleaned leeks and peeled onions finely. Melt the butter and add the leeks and onions. Let them soften, covered, for 15 minutes, without browning. Add the flour, stir in until absorbed, then gradually add hot stock as if you were making a Béchamel sauce. When there is no further danger of lumping, add all the stock and the wine, season and simmer for 30–35 minutes. Stir in the cream, cook gently for 5 minutes more and serve with crisply fried cubes of bacon.

Oatmeal cock-a-leekie (*for 4*)

This most famous of all Scottish soups requires cockerel stock (so specified because, presumably, the bones of the previously eaten bird were used to make it) and a number of 'leekies'. Chicken stock is what would be used today.

For 2 pints ($1\frac{1}{4}$l; 4 cups) of stock, the white part of 8 leeks, cut into small rings, is about the right amount. Sprinkle 2 tablespoons of oatmeal or porridge oats into the pot, and simmer until the vegetables and cereal are cooked.

Vichyssoise (*for 4–6 depending on appetites*)

Despite its French-sounding name, this soup was invented on an American liner and first served in mid-Atlantic.

6 leeks (lots of green), chopped	pepper
1 onion, finely chopped	5 or 6 potatoes, sliced
2oz (50g; $\frac{1}{4}$ cup) butter	1 pint ($\frac{3}{4}$l; 2 cups) milk
$1\frac{1}{2}$ pints (1l; 3 cups) chicken stock	nutmeg
salt	4 tablespoons cream
	3 tablespoons chopped chives

Sauté the leeks and onion in the butter and cook slowly, covered, for 5–10 minutes. Add the stock, salt and pepper and potatoes, and cook until the potatoes are soft. Sieve, mouli or put in the blender. Heat the milk with a touch of nutmeg and add to the soup. If eating it cold, chill, and add the cream and chives before serving. This is also good hot.

Welsh leek soup

Cut up 4 large floury potatoes in 3 pints (2l; 6 cups) of salted water. While they are on the boil, cook 4 big leeks, cut lengthways and then across into tiny segments, together with a chopped onion, in some butter. When they are quite soft, sprinkle with flour and stir what will be a leek-flavoured roux. Moisten with some potato water, stir until all is smooth, pour the mixture into the pan containing the potatoes, and simmer until the potatoes are almost mushy. Bind the liquid with 2 egg yolks, and serve.

Greek leeks

Boil some thin young leeks, trimmed but retaining as much of the green part as is still tightly rolled, in a little salted water. When they are almost soft, lift out the leeks and lay them in a shallow dish, side by side in a single layer. Thicken the leek liquor with a little cornflour stirred into cold water, and boil until transparent and thick enough to coat the spoon. Stir in 1 teaspoon of lemon juice and 1 tablespoon of olive oil. Decant the sauce over the leeks and let them cool, but do not chill – they should be eaten *chambré*.

Provençal leeks (*for 4*)

4 fine leeks	juice of ½ lemon
2 tablespoons olive oil	1 teaspoon shredded lemon
2 tomatoes	peel (the zest, not the
1 handful black olives	pith)

Cut the leeks into thumb-sized pieces, and simmer in the oil for 10 minutes in a shallow, covered, fireproof dish. Then add the quartered, skinned tomatoes and the other ingredients, season and cook for another 10 minutes. This dish can be eaten hot, as a vegetable, or cold, as a salad.

Leeks vinaigrette

Clean and trim some small leeks, allowing 4–6 per person. Bring a pan of salted water to the boil and drop them in. Let them cook until they are just tender. Put in a colander and let cold water splash over them for several minutes. In the meantime, mash a clove of garlic with salt, mix with Dijon mustard and plenty of freshly ground black pepper, add 1½ tablespoons wine vinegar and mix in thoroughly. Now add the oil, mixing gradually. You will need about 5 tablespoons, but taste it from time to time. Drain the leeks very thoroughly and lay them on a plate all pointing in the same direction. Pour on the dressing and turn them in it a couple of times.

Braised leeks

Start off by sweating the cut leeks, white parts and green, in butter over slow heat. Stir, season, and after 10 minutes or so, moisten with some clear stock, left-over gravy, or plain water.

Simmer, hermetically covered, for about 30 minutes, checking every now and then that the moisture has not entirely evaporated. (If this should be the case, add more liquid, but only a very little at a time – you are not preparing boiled leeks.) To finish off, add meat glaze, or a little extra butter which will make the leeks look glossy. This dish can also be prepared with the addition of skinned tomatoes.

Leeks in a creamy sauce

Use all the white part and every bit of green, discarding only the beard and the tips of the leaves that have wilted or discoloured. Cut into slices about the thickness of 2 fingers. Boil in a mixture of milk and water until tender and, using as much of this liquid as necessary, in another pan make a thick sauce based on a white roux. The sauce should be stiff enough to support the leeks, which should be folded rather than stirred in. Season, and add some top of the milk and a few tiny pieces of fresh butter to give the sauce the authentic velvet touch.

GARLIC *Allium sativum*

Normally this is used in such small amounts that its nutritive qualities, which are similar to those of the onion, are of little importance.

As ancient as the *leac*, and as well known to the Saxons, who called it *gar* (spear) *leac*, garlic over the centuries unhappily fell into disrepute in polite society. 'To be sure', said John Evelyn, 'tis not for ladies' Palats, nor for those who court them'; while another authority regrets that its smell was so dreaded by 'our little mistresses', since it was 'perhaps the most powerful remedy in existence against the vapours and nervous maladies to which they are subject.' And not only the vapours were thought to be cured by garlic. It was considered a powerful preventative of plague and other diseases: some sixteenth-century doctors would not have dreamt of venturing abroad without a few cloves of garlic in their pockets to protect themselves from the bad air (and presumably adding to the stench). There is a theory that garlic, eaten often enough in sufficient quantities, actually sweetens the breath and the blood, but this will hardly be borne out by the experience of travelling in crowded trains or buses in Italy or the South of France, where garlic consumption could hardly be greater. One thing is certain; it makes little difference whether garlic, the *sine qua non* of all the most delicious Provençal dishes, is used discreetly or liberally. No matter whether you have eaten a *soupçon* or a spoonful, your friends will know it; but they will hardly be in a position to complain if they have shared the meal.

Garlic soup

Cook 12 skinned cloves of garlic in 2 pints (1¼l; 4 cups) of water, together with seasoning and a bouquet of fresh herbs, for 20 minutes. Season and strain, boiling hot, straight into the bowls in each of which you have placed some toasted

Garlic
Allium sativum

slices of buttered French bread thickly heaped with grated cheese. The bread will swell up, the cheese will melt, and the flavour will be surprisingly delicate.

Garlic bread

Slice a French loaf diagonally into thick slices, stopping short of the bottom crust. Thickly butter each side of each slice with butter in which garlic has been pounded; 4oz (110g; ½ cup) of salted butter and 1 mashed clove of garlic will do for 1 long loaf. Wrap the bread in foil, and place on the centre shelf of a fairly hot oven. In 15 minutes, the crust will be crustier and the crumb will have absorbed the flavoured butter. Serve hot with hors d'oeuvre or with soups – it adds glamour to any savoury first course.

Aïoli

This most famous of all Provençal sauces is a mayonnaise made in the usual way, except that 3 or 4 crushed cloves of garlic are combined with the egg yolk before the oil is added. It is most usually served with fish, hot or cold. It can also be an accompaniment to various mixtures of fish and/or vegetables, when it becomes *aïoli garni*. Such a mixture may consist of cold cooked French beans, fennel, little onions, salad potatoes cooked in their jackets, artichokes, and whatever else may be to hand. Hard-boiled shelled eggs, in wedges, may be added – the point is to make as attractive an arrangement as possible.

Stuffed eggs

Hard-boil at least as many eggs as there are people to feed.

Shell and halve lengthways, scoop out the yolks, and mash in a bowl with mustard, oil, seasoning and a small crushed clove of garlic. The mixture should be smooth and fairly stiff. Spooned back on to the eggs in little mounds, this is a good dish to prepare for a cold buffet lunch or supper.

Green salad with garlic

Whether to use a garlic press, or simply to crush garlic cloves under the point of a knife, or whether to squash them with the aid of a fork, has for so long been argued that no useful purpose is served in continuing the debate. It is now agreed that the difference lies in the varying amounts of juices and oils released. Depending on how vivaciously you mean to animate the salad (to paraphrase that eighteenth-century *bon viveur*, Sydney Smith), you can run the gamut from rubbing the sides of the bowl with the cut edge of a garlic clove, to incorporating a mashed-up clove, together with parsley, chives and dill in a green Vinaigrette. Or you could spread with pounded garlic a small slice of toasted French bread, soaked in olive oil, and place this face down on the bottom of the dish; the aroma will permeate the salad without any direct contact between the leaves and the bulb.

Roast whole heads of garlic

Arrange several whole corms of fresh garlic, say 2 per person, around a roasting chicken or leg of lamb. When the bird or joint is done, so is the garlic.

You eat it by pressing the base between your fingers; the garlic, which has been reduced to a rich mush, will squirt into your mouth.

CABBAGES & KIN

Cabbage
Brassica oleracea

Cabbage is good for you. All members of the family, from Brussels sprouts to broccoli, contain iron and vitamins. Cabbage and kale contain iron and other inorganic mineral substances and vitamins A, B and C; a helping has less than 25 calories.

Even the water in which cabbage was boiled was considered the universal panacea in the Ancient World. Taken internally, or applied externally, it was thought to alleviate all known diseases, to dissipate drunkenness and remove freckles; such were its health-giving properties that even to chop or slice it made one feel stronger at once.

Much was said about its benefits, less about its culinary values. In the opinion of one eighteenth-century Frenchman, it was the excessive eating of cabbage that made his luckless English counterpart 'by nature a dull animal'. 'Warmed-up cabbage wears out the poor magister's life', said Juvenal; and certainly cabbage dishes abound in the earliest English cookery books. In the fifteenth century it was 'served forth' dressed with saffron and 'gobbetys of marrow bonys', but not, one hopes, in high summer, since a sixteenth-century author firmly writes, '. . . if thou desirest to die, eat cabbage in August.' Culpeper, referring in some wonderment to the Romans' enthusiasm for cabbage, adds that he does not know 'what metal their bodies were made of', and calls them 'as windy a meat as can be eaten, unless you eat bag-pipes'.

CABBAGE *Brassica oleracea*

Although cabbage was eaten all over the world for thousands of years, it never quite made the grade in high cuisine. Louis XIV's large kitchen garden was devoid of red cabbage, to the chagrin of his German sister-in-law, who had some seeds sent from her homeland and introduced it to the royal menu. In England a great variety of cabbage existed from the sixteenth century onwards; but, sadly, it was in English kitchens that cabbage was brought into disrepute. There was, and still is, overcooking in too much water in closed pans, with either insufficient draining or too much squashing down of the soggy mess into tasteless slabs: young cabbage lost its attraction as a green vegetable, and mature cabbage lost its satisfying character as part of the robust dishes for which it is uniquely suitable.

Basic treatment

Remove the stalk and the outer wilted leaves. Unless your recipe calls for an entire head of cabbage, cut it into quarters and remove the core. Strip kale leaves from the stalks, and remove the tough central ribs. Then shred or chop or use in wedges as the recipe dictates. Cooking times vary; 5–10 minutes in a *small* quantity of boiling salted water in an uncovered pan will be quite enough to transform green cabbage into a bright and delicate spring vegetable; while 1–2 hours will not be too much for braising a red cabbage. It very much depends not just on the age of the vegetable, but also on the nature of the dish.

Garbure

Slice 1 cabbage, 8 potatoes, 3 carrots and 1 stalk of celery, and put them in a large pot with some cooked haricot beans and a piece of boiling bacon. Pour on 2 pints (1¼l; 4 cups) of cold water and bring to the boil. Put in 2 cloves of garlic. Bring to the boil, then simmer for 1 hour. Remove the meat, cut it from the bone in chunks and return it to the soup with the shredded cabbage. Mix well together, and cook for another 45 minutes to 1 hour.

Soupe au choux (*for 4–6*)

This is the ideal dish to make the day after you have cooked some ham or a piece of gammon, because the flavour of the cooking liquid harmonizes beautifully with the cabbage.

Bring 4 pints (2½l; 8 cups) of the stock to the boil, add half a firm green cabbage, washed and cut into small shreds, 3 potatoes peeled and cut into cubes, and 1 slice of bacon or gammon, also cut into small pieces.

Simmer with a tilted lid on the pan for 45 minutes. Season. Serve sprinkled with grated Gruyère or Emmenthal cheese. If you choose to add cream, it makes the soup a little more refined, which is not necessarily a good thing; this is a simple, good-hearted country soup, which also works quite well without the bacon stock.

Hot slaw (*for 4–6*)

½ hard white cabbage, about 1lb (450g)	1 tablespoon butter
¼ small red cabbage, about ½lb (225g)	½ teaspoon salt
	2 tablespoons sugar
4 tablespoons vinegar	2 tablespoons water
1 teaspoon mustard	2 egg yolks
	4 tablespoons sour cream

Take off the outside leaves, cut away the stalks and shred the cabbages very finely. If, at the cost of losing some vitamins and minerals, you soak the shreds in two bowls of very cold water, one for the white cabbage and one for the red, this makes them very crisp and improves their colour.

In the top of a double boiler mix all the remaining ingredients with the exception of the sour cream. Thicken the mixture over gently boiling water, stirring constantly or at least frequently, until it is the consistency of thin cream. Stir a spoonful or two of this mixture into the sour cream and then return it to the top of the double boiler and heat through, stirring, until you have a hot, creamy sauce.

Meanwhile, drain the cabbage, mix the two colours in a bowl, pour on the hot dressing, mix and serve immediately.

This salad is very good eaten cold as well as hot (or warm, as it actually is by the time the cabbage has cooled the sauce). If you want it really hot you can heat the sliced cabbage gently in the dressing, but the cabbage loses its texture. Serve it with frankfurters, with hefty slices of fried ham, or with hamburgers.

Whole stuffed cabbage (*for 4–6 according to size of cabbage*)

This is a fairly spectacular dish, for which you halve the cabbage crossways about one-third up. Plunge the vegetable into a pan of boiling water for 3 or 4 minutes to make it pliable, and drain it well (saving some of the water), cut surface down. Carefully scoop out the middle to make a cavity for the stuffing. If you have a large cabbage, take 4 heaped tablespoons of raw minced beef, 2 slices of bread soaked in milk and pressed out, 1 egg, and the scoopings from the cabbage, finely chopped and fried in butter together with a chopped onion. Mix well and spoon into both halves of hollow. Dot with butter. Replace the top half 'lid' of the cabbage and tie some string round both halves. Put the whole thing into a fireproof dish, and pour the remains of the butter in which the onion and the shredded cabbage have been fried, and enough of the blanching water to make the liquid come one-third up the cabbage head. Place on the middle shelf of the oven preheated to Reg 4/350°F and cook for about 1 hour or until the stuffing is cooked. Cut the string, sprinkle with paprika, and dish up with boiled potatoes.

Stuffed cabbage leaves (*for 4–6*)

1 firm fresh cabbage (white or green)	skinned and chopped
1 large onion, coarsely chopped	4 tablespoons long-grain rice, cooked
1lb (450g) left-over meat, minced	2 tablespoons chopped mint
1lb (450g) tomatoes,	salt
	cayenne pepper
	a little butter

Before you can stuff cabbage leaves, they must first be softened so that they can be folded around the stuffing. To do this, simply cut them one at a time through their stems and peel them off carefully; drop them into a large pan of boiling salted water for 5 minutes and then cool them quickly under cold running water. Drain them well.

Soften the chopped onion in butter. Mix together all the ingredients to make a stuffing, put 1 tablespoon of the mixture on each leaf and roll them up, pushing the ends in with your fingers, to prevent the stuffing emerging during the cooking.

Put a layer of left-over blanched outer leaves in the bottom of a saucepan, place the stuffed leaves on top, closely packed together, dot with butter, and cover with more outer leaves. Weight them with a plate, add a scant $\frac{1}{2}$ pint ($\frac{1}{4}$l; 1 cup) of water or light stock and simmer, with the pan covered, for 50 minutes to 1 hour, checking from time to time to see if more liquid is needed. Serve very hot with sour cream or plain yoghurt.

Buttered white cabbage

On a medium heat cook a roughly chopped cabbage and 2 cloves of garlic in a little milk, until the vegetable is soft but not mushy – you are not making porridge but a dish with some bite to it. As soon as the cabbage seems done, increase the heat, stirring thoroughly so that the bottom layer of cabbage does not stick to the pot. When all the excess liquid has evaporated, stir in as much butter as you can bring yourself to use; 2 tablespoons, added gradually, is the minimum. When every bit of cabbage is coated and buttery, add a dollop of cream. This way of serving cabbage, which is a revelation of its delicate flavour, is particularly good with mutton.

White cabbage salad (*for 4*)

An excellent winter salad, not only because it tastes fresh and sharp, but because it contains a tremendous amount of vitamin C (which helps to keep colds at bay).
Finely shred 1 small white cabbage, grate 1 thick slice of celeriac and 2 apples, and chop 1 very small onion. Sprinkle the apple with lemon juice to prevent it from turning brown,

and mix all the ingredients together. Add 1 handful of sultanas, previously soaked, and a few chopped nuts – hazelnuts, walnuts, or almonds. Dress with mayonnaise, sour cream, or yoghourt with a spoonful of French mustard added. This salad is good with cheese, eaten after a thick soup.

Polish cabbage with noodles (*for 4–6 as a main course*)

1 large green cabbage	2–3 onions
$\frac{1}{2}$lb (225g) noodles	pepper
butter	salt

Bring to the boil 2 pans of well-salted water. Quarter the cabbage, cut away the thicker part of the core, wash the quarters well and drop them into one pan. In the other pan put the noodles, stirring them to prevent them from sticking together. Melt a good lump of butter in a shallow pan and soften the onions, peeled and cut downwards into slivers, until tender and transparent. When the cabbage is just tender drain it very well, cut it up a little with a knife and add another lump of butter. Add the onions, together with their butter, and let everything sit over a low heat for 10 minutes or so, stirring from time to time so that any extra liquid evaporates. This makes the final result more mellow. Meanwhile, drain the cooked noodles very well, stir them into the cabbage and season extravagantly with freshly ground black pepper, and with salt if it is needed.

Red cabbage (*to eat with the Christmas goose or its leftovers*)

Shred a nice firm red cabbage, chop an onion, and stir them about in a pan in which some goose-dripping, or, failing this, some white fat has been melted. When all is evenly coated, add a dash of vinegar, which will immediately brighten up the cabbage. Stir, cover, and cook on the lowest possible heat while you pare, core and slice a cooking apple or two. Add to the vegetables, stir again, and if there is less than 1in (2·5cm) of liquid, top up with water and/or a dash of red wine. Season with salt, add 2 lumps of sugar and a small handful of currants. If there is any cranberry sauce left over, put that in as well – the idea is to achieve a sweet/sour/savoury flavour. This will slowly develop in the cooking process, during which the cabbage will lose its aggressive mauve look and turn a subtle shade of plum. Theoretically, as soon as this second colour change has occurred – it will take about 1 hour – the cabbage is ready for the table, but in practice the longer it cooks the better it is, in fact it is one of the few dishes that tastes better reheated than the first time round.

Red caraway cabbage (*for 4–6*)

Wash and shred 1 red cabbage and cook in 4 tablespoons of butter or oil in a covered pan for a few minutes. Slice 2 large cooking apples and 3 onions. In a casserole put a layer of cabbage, then one of apples, one of onions, and so on. Sprinkle each layer with salt, pepper and a pinch of cinnamon and nutmeg, and a generous pinch of caraway seeds. Sprinkle some brown sugar on the top and pour over the dish 2 wine glasses of liquor, one glass of red wine with a dash of vinegar, and one wine glass of hot water. Cover and cook slowly in a moderate oven (Reg 4/350°F) until tender, for up to 2 hours.

Cabbage and diced bacon (*for 4–6*)

Place a finely shredded white cabbage in a colander and rinse it under the cold tap. Put it in a pan with a knob of butter; no extra water beyond what clings to the cabbage is needed. Stir it over a medium heat and increase the heat as the cabbage shreds collapse, so that the liquid evaporates. The whole cooking operation will not take more than 5 minutes. Set aside, and fry over gentle heat 3 thick, diced slices of streaky bacon. When the bacon cubes have turned golden at the edges, add a chopped onion. When this is just coloured, but not brown, stir in the cabbage until it is heated through. This dish needs an accompaniment of floury boiled potatoes.

Choucroute

Choucroute, the national dish of Alsace-Lorraine, is cabbage which has been shredded and packed into a wooden keg with layers of salt and caraway seeds. A little water transforms the salt into a brine in which the cabbage ferments, and in which it assumes its distinctive sour taste: *sauerkraut* is its German name. Do-it-yourself makers of *sauerkraut* must cover the keg with a cloth and as long as active fermentation is taking place, they must, once weekly, remove the scum that rises to the surface and top up the tub of salted water.

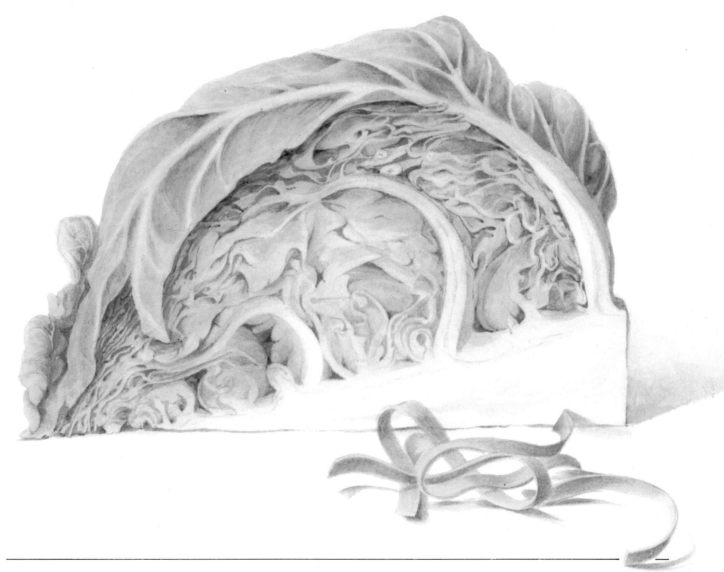

How to grow brassica

Cabbages

Cabbages can be sown, according to variety, in spring for the summer, in summer for the winter, and in late summer for the spring, so they are all-the-year-round good value. Sow summer cabbages in spring, ¾in (1·5cm) deep in a flat seed bed, and plant out the seedlings 18in (45cm) apart each way, in early summer, in good rich ground. Hoe and water well. Green, white and red cabbages and Savoys are sown from mid- to late summer and transplanted at the end of the season. The seedlings should be planted 9in (23cm) apart if they are to be eaten as spring greens, and 18in (45cm) if they are to grow big and hearty.

Brussels sprouts

Brussels sprouts are raised in a seed bed like cabbages, and then planted out. There is one important point to remember: they need planting firmly (the soil compressed round them) to produce tight button sprouts and not the blown-up little cabbages which are so disappointing. They also need a long, steady growing period. Seedlings are usually put out in early summer, in succession so that you do not get a lot the same size all at once. Plant them in showery weather; if dry, water them well. The plants should be sturdy and about 4–6in (10–15cm) tall with 3ft (1m) between them as they like plenty of space. (You can save some of this space by putting some quick-growing plants between the rows.) As they reach maturity some of the leaves will go yellow and these must be removed; take off the lower leaves too to help the sprouts develop. Pick regularly, and always from the bottom. The succulent Brussels tops are eaten last, at the very end of the season.

Cauliflower

Cauliflowers are divided into summer ones, and winter (which used to be known as winter broccoli). Summer cauliflowers can be sown under glass in winter for very early heads, but the majority are sown in a seed bed in spring to early summer; winter cauliflowers are sown at the same time. Remember that a succession is only achieved by sowing different varieties. Cauliflowers, almost more than other plants, have been bred to mature at specified times of the year; careful sowing and choosing can give you supplies the year round. They are unfortunately the most difficult of the brassica. They like good rich soil and plenty of water and should be planted out, as early, shallowly and firmly as possible. Give them plenty of room, and try to put them in a sunny but sheltered position. When the white curds begin to show, pull off a leaf and put it over the plant for protection.

Broccoli

Sprouting broccoli is a very useful winter crop. Different varieties can give you shoots to eat from late summer to spring. Hardier than cauliflowers, broccoli needs no protection except from pigeons who like them as much as we do. Sow in late spring, then first to 6in (15cm) and finally to 2ft (60cm) apart.

Whether choucroute is homemade, bought loose, freshly fermented from a giant tub at a delicatessen store, or is in tins, it can be eaten hot or cold, simply warmed up or prepared as follows.

Melt 2 tablespoons of goose or pork fat in a heavy fireproof casserole. Add 2 tablespoons of water, 1lb (450g) of well-drained choucroute, 1 sliced apple and 1 chopped onion. Cover well and boil gently for 45 minutes. Just before serving, add 1 glass of white wine (in Alsace they add kirsch). Dish up with smoked sausage of the frankfurter variety, or with pigs' trotters or gammon, or braised gamebirds.

BRUSSELS SPROUTS
Brassica oleracea bullata gemmifera

These contain vitamins A, B, E and K, and masses of vitamin C to ward off winter chills. They are in the middle group for calories with about 40 in a helping.

Named after the Belgian capital, this member of the Brassica family has been grown in the Netherlands for many centuries. Flemish refugees from the Spanish Inquisition brought them to England, where they have been grown ever since, and have been as ill-treated by cooks as the rest of the cabbage tribe. Young and firm, and not overcooked, they have the flavour of fresh nuts. Old, tousle-headed and cooked to extinction, they taste like dishwater, and have the texture of a wet mop.

Basic treatment

Tight freshly picked buds do not need to be criss-crossed at the base of the stem, and need no longer than 5 minutes in boiling water. Older sprouts do need to be so incised, but even they should not be boiled longer than 12 minutes at the outside.

Sprouts, old or young, should always be properly drained, and returned to the heat afterwards so that the excess liquid evaporates. They are eaten simply with fresh butter, or with browned butter with breadcrumbs. They are also good *au jus*, with the addition of some good clear gravy. Some people like them with Béchamel sauce or with fried bacon, and they are classic companions to chestnuts, either served separately, or carefully mixed – this is particularly delicious with turkey or gamebirds. They can also be puréed, and used in cream soups or in soufflés.

Bubble and Squeak

This nursery dish is nicest – for grown-ups as well as for children – when little Brussels sprouts take the place of the usual cold 'greens'.

Use two-thirds of cooked potatoes to one-third of sprouts (or greens), a knob of lard or dripping, and seasoning. Dice the potatoes. If the sprouts are tiny, leave them whole; if as large as walnuts or bigger, slice them thickly. (Greens should be fairly finely chopped.) Mix the vegetables in a bowl so

Cauliflower
Brassica oleracea botrytis

that they are evenly distributed. Heat a knob of lard at medium temperature in a shallow pan small enough to allow the vegetables to stand 1in or so (about 2·5cm) high when they are compressed. Put the vegetables in the pan and press them down to form a solid cake. Lower the heat. Do not stir them about – the object is to let a solid crust form at the bottom. A little more dripping can, if necessary, be carefully inserted from the side; it will find its own way to the bottom. With a spatula, turn the slab after 7–10 minutes, and repeat the procedure until you have a golden crisp cake with a soft centre.

CAULIFLOWER *Brassica oleracea botrytis*

This contains vitamins A, B and a lot of C. It is rich in potassium and phosphorous, and low in calories – less than 25 a helping.

Cauliflowers, which Mark Twain was to call 'nothing but cabbages with a college education', were mentioned in the earliest gardening books. Originally, they were no larger than tennis balls enclosed in enormous leaves. They have been cultivated beyond all recognition; though, ironically, freezing firms are now experimenting with dwarfish golf-ball cauliflowers for convenient packaging. But cauliflowers larger than men's heads are the pride of every vegetable show, and the first Englishman to breed one of reasonable size in the seventeenth century was clearly celebrated for this feat, since the vegetable is carved on his tombstone.

He would certainly turn in his grave at the indignities to which his pride and joy has been subjected. The chalk-white floury blanket under which too many cauliflowers make their anaemic appearance has almost ruined its reputation, but although the cauliflower can be a very boring vegetable, with the help of something extra it can excel.

Basic treatment

Cut off all wilting outer leaves. If to be cooked whole, leave a few of the tender green leaves around the stalk – they make the cauliflower look fresher and more appetizing – and cut a cross in the base of the stalk. Alternatively, divide the cauliflower into separate flowerets. Wash in cold water. Cooking times again vary, but 15 minutes in boiling water will be the maximum, even for a large dense head.

Cheese sauce is the best-known addition, but there are many alternatives. Try fresh breadcrumbs, fried golden and sprinkled over cauliflower which has been lightly cooked and broken into flowerets. Or serve it in a border of rice – potatoes do not look happy in the company of cauliflower – but rice looks nice, especially if the cauliflower sits in the centre of a ring, and is served with deeply coloured, highly flavoured, creamy tomato sauce based on a pale roux to which a generous amount of Italian tomato purée has been added. Rice-ringed cauliflower, surrounded by halved hard-boiled eggs for cheering colour, is very good with a smooth beige-brown mustard sauce, for which plenty of Dijon mustard is needed.

Cauliflower soup

Cook a large cauliflower in a mixture of milk and water until it is soft. In another large saucepan, make a pale roux. Use the liquid in which the cauliflower has cooked to make a soup of the consistency of thin cream. Cut the cauliflower in two, passing one half through a sieve and into the soup. Divide the other half into little sprigs, and add, together with a dash of cream. Season, and serve with tiny golden croûtons.

Cauliflower with dip

Raw cauliflower, if it is really crisp and fresh, has a delicious taste reminiscent of walnuts. Divide a fine head into small flowerets. Arrange these on a round plate in the centre of which is a shallow bowl filled with *aïoli* – a sharp mayonnaise strongly flavoured with garlic.

Cauliflower cheese (*for 4*)

Properly prepared, this dish is a far cry from the mushy abomination that often goes by this name.

Break or cut 1 large cauliflower into flowerets and drop them into a large pan of boiling salted water. Let them cook for 6 minutes – they must be rather crisp. Drain them and put them into an oval earthenware gratin dish or some other fireproof dish. Pour ½ pint (¼l; 1 cup) cream, seasoned with salt and pepper, over them. Smother everything with grated cheese and cook rapidly in the top of the oven until brown and crisp on top (about 20 minutes).

Alternatively, cook the cauliflower in boiling water to which some milk has been added. Save the liquor when you drain the vegetable and use to make a smooth, thick white sauce based on a white roux. There should be a generous addition of grated cheese to the sauce when it is drawn off

the flame. Pour the sauce over the cauliflower in its fireproof dish, tipping it this way and that so that it sinks between the flowerets. Top with a layer of grated cheese, dot with butter and brown under heat until the surface is nicely flecked and speckled.

Cauliflower and anchovy salad

Drain a cauliflower after cooking, and carefully separate into flowerets. Put these in your salad dish, and before they have cooled, drench them in a Vinaigrette sauce. Allow to go quite cold, and arrange a lattice of filleted anchovies on top. Accompanied by hard-boiled eggs, this makes a pleasant cold dish for lunch, and is, indeed, a classical one; it is mentioned by a royal seventeenth-century traveller – although in a spirit of criticism, since a single small cauliflower, 6 eggs and 6 anchovies had to be shared by a party of eight.

Cauliflower fritters

Divide a cauliflower into flowerets. Dip these in batter, and deep fry in oil. Drain them on kitchen paper and sprinkle with chopped parsley. Serve with a sauce made with a few chopped mushrooms, some crushed garlic, and 2 tomatoes cut into thick slices, all gently simmered in oil for 5 minutes or so.

Batter for fritters

4oz (110g) flour	¼ pint (⅛l; ½ cup) lukewarm
pinch of salt	water
3 tablespoons melted butter	1 egg white

Start making the batter about 2 hours before it is needed. In a bowl mix the flour, a pinch of salt, and the melted butter, then add the water gradually until you have a thickish creamy mixture. Let it stand in a cool place. At the last moment, beat the egg white to soft peaks and fold into the batter.

KOHLRABI *Brassica oleracea caulorapa*

It is well worth having a little of this Brassica which produces a decorative bulb on the stem surmounted by a crown of leaves. Sow in summer, *in situ* (not in a seed bed as with others of this family), and thin to 6in (15cm) apart. It is most important to cut and eat them when they are no bigger than a tennis ball, and the crop must be grown quickly or it will be tough and woody (when, however, it is still good made into a creamy soup). Young kohlrabi are eaten simply with butter, or with a white sauce flecked with chopped herbs.

BROCCOLI *Brassica oleracea botrytis cauliflora*

It is rich in vitamins A and C, calcium, iron and phosphorus. Plain-boiled with no great dollops of butter or Hollandaise sauce, a helping of broccoli contains about 40 calories.

Broccoli
Brassica oleracea botrytis cauliflora

Basic treatment

There are various types of broccoli: some have deep green, stout stems with pale, succulent, slippery insides and green tops (called 'curds'); others look like cauliflowers with purple heads which, however, turn green when they are cooked. Broccoli should be plunged into boiling water for not more than 6–8 minutes; the stem variety is used *en branche*, and the cauliflower sort is separated into flowerets.

Broccoli is most usually eaten with Hollandaise, and sometimes with Béarnaise, sauce.

Broccoli and cauliflower

For this dish, cooked whole cauliflower forms the centre-piece. Broccoli flowerets, which must on no account be overcooked, are arranged in a garland round it, and the dish is eaten with Hollandaise sauce.

Broccoli with lemon butter

Cook the broccoli so that the vegetable still has some bite about it. Drain and place in a serving dish; keep warm. Hard-boil 3 eggs. Whisk together over a low flame 4oz (110g; ½ cup) of butter, the juice of half a lemon, and seasoning. Remove from the heat. Chop the eggs finely. Amalgamate them with the lemon butter, and pour over the broccoli.

Broccoli cheese

Put cooked broccoli into a fireproof dish. Mix 2 eggs, slightly beaten with ¾ pint (½l; 1½ cup) of milk, a little lemon juice and about 6 tablespoons of grated cheese – any hard yellow cheese would be suitable. Season this mixture, pour over the broccoli, and place the dish in a pan of hot water in a medium oven. It will have set within about 30 minutes.

TUBERS

Potato
Solanum tuberosum

Whether it was Sir Walter Ralegh, Sir Francis Drake, the geographer Thomas Herriot, or a Spanish monk called Hieronymus Cardian who first brought the potato to Europe from its native South America – and each has been credited with its introduction – the fact is that we owe its popularization to an eighteenth-century French agronomist, Antoine-Auguste Parmentier.

Ralegh's potatoes, alas, got off to an inauspicious start. He had sent some plants to Queen Elizabeth I with detailed instructions, and soon potatoes were seen growing on the banks of the Thames. The Elizabethans, who were fond of sweet potatoes – 'the inside eateth like an apple but is more delicious than any apple sugred' – did not take kindly to the other sort. Matters were not helped by a banquet at which potatoes featured in every course – stalks, leaves and all – and which was followed by stomach-aches. After this, the potato languished in spite of various efforts to reintroduce it.

Gerard, who received some potatoes direct from Virginia, sang its praises in 1597; 'a pleasant dish . . . whether they be baked in hot ashes, or boiled and eaten with oile,

vinegar or pepper, or dressed in any other way by the hand of anyone cunning in cookerie.' He sang in vain.

A volume arguing its case, entitled 'England's Happiness Increased or a Pure and Easie Remedy against all succeeding Dear Years by plantation of the roots called potatoes' was published towards the end of the seventeenth century, but to no avail. The French, far from agreeing that the potato was, in Gerard's words, 'equal in wholesomeness and salubrity to the batata (yam)', credited it with enfeebling properties and, fearing leprosy, in some districts banned its cultivation.

Another century passed and then came Parmentier, whose name still features in many potato dishes. Realizing, as others had done before him, that the denigrated potato was a valuable food in times of scarcity (he listed it with horse-chestnuts, acorns, the roots of bryony, iris, gladioli and couchgrass), he published its chemical analysis in 1773. In 1787, when the grain harvest had failed, he was granted permission to put an acre of poor land near Paris under potato, which successfully grew against all expectations.

People were still unprepared to accept this new food, but when Parmentier hit upon the idea of putting the field under military guard by day, and leaving it unguarded by night, the Parisians responded as he had expected. Predictably they descended upon it under cover of darkness, carried away what they now felt sure was a precious crop.

The treatment dished out to potatoes in French *haute cuisine* ranges from simple steaming or boiling – needless to say, this is called *à l'anglaise* – to potato slices, deep-fried in two separate pans of fat, one 350°F (175°C) and the second 400°F (200°C) which makes them puff up into little spheres and turns them into *pommes soufflées*.

Raw potatoes, cut into matchsticks and deep-fried, become *pommes alumettes*; as thin, but twice as long, they become *paille* or straw potatoes. Pont-Neuf potatoes are cut thicker and squarer than chips, and Bénédictine potatoes are little fried turban shapes for which a special cutter is needed.

Olive shaped raw potato balls – made with the help of a special scoop – either parboiled and finished in butter, or cooked in butter only, are *pommes châteaux*, *pommes fondantes*, or *pommes noisettes*, depending on softness, and on whether herbs are added.

An absolutely delicious way of preparing potatoes, although perhaps one of the most fattening, is to cook them *à la crème* – that is, parboiled in water, then skinned and sliced, and finished in milk with a dollop of fresh cream added at the last minute.

Mashed potatoes – peeled, cooked, drained and puréed with a fork or masher, and then whipped up with hot milk and butter into snowy peaks – are hard to beat, but this lily, too, is sometimes gilded: the addition of diced ham, chopped green peppers and herbs makes *pommes Biarritz*; extra butter and the yolk of an egg produces *pommes duchesse*, which usually appears as a crusty frill, piped around the top of gratin dishes.

Pommes Anna are made with thin round slices of raw potatoes, arranged in a thick layer, moistened with melted butter, and cooked in the oven. The addition of grated cheese and a bit of nutmeg makes them *pommes voisin*; but again, cream and a little garlic and stock are added instead of the cheese, and they become *pommes dauphinoise*.

POTATO *Solanum tuberosum*

The potato is one of the most valuable and nutritious of vegetables. It provides vitamins B and C and is a good source of carbohydrate. High in calories, one medium-sized boiled potato contains about 100. Most of the goodness of potatoes lies directly under the skin, so whenever possible, do not peel or scrape them at all; they are easy to slip out of their skins after cooking.

When unpeeled potatoes cool down after cooking, the skin sometimes becomes rather clinging, but it is simple to remove if the potato is rinsed under the hot tap at the start of the operation.

Boiling times for potatoes can vary from the usual 20 minutes. Very freshly picked small new potatoes may not need more than 5 minutes in the water, and should moreover go into the pot only when the water has reached boiling point.

In the case of peeled potatoes, peel them thinly, and do not let them sit about or they will blacken. (If they *have* to wait, put them into a bowl of water.) Finish them by draining off the cooking water (which some people like to use as stock because of the nutrients) and then placing a folded towel over the potatoes in the pan. Replace the lid, and let the towel absorb the steam – your potatoes will look handsomer as a result. (The towel can also to some degree dry out soggy potatoes, but for this rescue operation you need to keep the pan over a very low heat.)

When you sauté potatoes, or French fry them (after blotting the cut pieces with a towel so that they go into the hot fat or oil as dry as possible), their colour will tell you when they are done.

Blended soups

From a puréed potato base, many delicious soups can be prepared. For a Flemish potage, the mash is moistened to soup consistency, and mixed with Brussels sprouts passed through a sieve or mouli and garnished with small cooked sprouts. Potatoes and leeks go well together, as do potatoes and onions, potatoes and celeriac or any of the roots. For marbled soup, add some cooked chopped spinach to a basic creamy potato soup *after* it has been decanted into a tureen or bowl, drawing it carefully over the surface for a streaky effect.

Chervil potato soup (*for 4*)

1½lb (675g) potatoes	1 dessertspoon flour,
2 onions	blended in milk
just over 1 pint (¾l; 2¼ cups) white stock	1 slice fried bread chervil
cream	

Slice the potatoes and onions and simmer in the stock until soft. Put through a sieve or mouli, or in the blender, and return to the heat. Add the blended flour and milk and bring to the boil. Pour into hot bowls, and add the cream, small crispy bits of fried bread and a generous teaspoon of chopped chervil to each bowl.

Warm potato salad (*for 6*)

Cook 1½lb (675g) of potatoes in their jackets for 20 minutes. While they boil, make a salad dressing in a large bowl, using 6 tablespoons of oil, 3 of vinegar, 1 of mustard, 1 of finely chopped onion, and a handful of parsley chopped extremely fine. When the potatoes are just done – they should not be overcooked – drain and rinse under the cold tap, so that they can be handled. Skin and slice thinly into the bowl with the dressing – the interior of the potatoes will still be steaming. Make sure that they are all coated with dressing, but mix the salad carefully so that the slices do not break. Serve luke-warm. This salad can, of course, be eaten cold, but should never be chilled.

Bonne femme (*for 6*)

The soup of the 'good woman' and always a favourite.

Cook 4 sliced carrots and 3 leeks (as much of the green spear as possible) gently in some butter. Add 10 potatoes peeled and diced, about 2 pints (1¼l; 4 cups) of liquid – stock or water – and a little salt. Cook quite slowly for 30 minutes, then mouli or sieve finely. Season with salt and pepper, add a little cream and sprinkle with parsley and some tiny croûtons.

Mayonnaise potato salad

Cut 1lb (450g) of cooled, peeled, cooked potatoes into slices, dress in a Vinaigrette and carefully mix with 6 tablespoons of mayonnaise which has been mixed with 2 or 3 tablespoons of chopped parsley. The mayonnaise will become runny as it combines with the dressing, but this is all to the good; dry potato salad is not worth eating.

Potato and tomato pie (*for 6*)

Cook 12 potatoes in their jackets, cool, skin and slice. Slice 6 large raw tomatoes. Chop 1 large onion, and grate a chunk of hard cheese. Chop 2 leaves of basil. In a greased fireproof dish place a layer of potato, and on top of that a layer of tomato. Sprinkle with onion, cheese and basil, and continue, finishing with a tomato layer. Pour a wine glass of oil over the lot, and cook in a hot oven until the top is nicely browned.

Fennel potato pie

Peel and slice potatoes according to the number of hungry people, reckoning 2 per person. Butter a baking dish and put in a layer of potato slices, pepper, salt and fennel seed. Dot with butter. Go on layering and finish by pouring over a well-seasoned white sauce, or cream, or milk in which an egg has been beaten. Slices of bacon are good in this, or a little sliced or grated cheese. Bake in a moderate oven (Reg 4/ 350°F) for about 1 hour.

Onion and potato omelette (*for 4*)

This is a sort of *tortilla*, but it requires fewer potatoes and more eggs than the real thing, and is cooked over a less fierce heat and in far less oil than is used in Spain.

Peel and boil 4 potatoes. Chop 1 onion finely and soften in a very little oil and butter without browning. Add the cubed cooked potatoes and heat them thoroughly, even brown them slightly. Beat 6 eggs briefly with salt and pepper, make the omelette as usual and add the potato and onion mixture, spreading it all over, halfway through the cooking. Serve with a green salad.

How to grow potatoes

The land for potatoes should be dug over in the early winter and left rough. Try to get hold of some of the waxy salad potatoes, as these make the best salads and chips. Seed tuber should be the size of a hen's egg; if larger, cut them lengthways just before planting. Put the tubers in shallow trays to sprout in the dark; ideally, the sprouted shoots should be green and not allowed to get long and weedy, they should not be more than 2in (5cm) long. The sprouted tubers are put carefully into 3–4in (8–10cm) furrows running north and south. Mixed fertilizer is a good idea at planting time. When the plants are 6–9in (15–23cm) high, earth should be pulled up round them with a hoe, and again in two to three weeks. Spraying against blight should be done in the early summer when needed; the main-crop varieties for winter and storing are lifted in the very late summer – or even earliest winter – and dried on the ground for a few hours before being stored in boxes of sand or peat or in clamps or paperpacks. The texture of potatoes, whether floury (for mashing) or waxy, can be affected by differences in soil and climate, so find out which varieties are the most successful in your area. Potatoes are very amenable and will grow anywhere; a few in an odd corner will give you some meals and do the soil good. You can even try growing some in large pots or buckets, or in plastic bags filled with compost in a greenhouse or shed. They are also the best ground-clearing crop: if you have a patch of soil which has not been cultivated and therefore hard work to dig up, potatoes will do the job for you. Place them *on* the ground, cover with straw, lawn-mowing or even crumpled strips of black polythene. In no time, the top growth of the potato will show above the cover and the roots will penetrate even cement-like topsoil.

1. Shoots should be green and sturdy – not pale and weedy

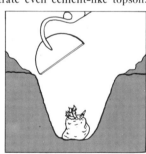

2. Plant the sprouted tuber into furrow, draw earth over it with a hoe

3. Fully fill up trench using a spade

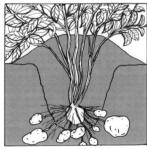

4. Earth up so that potatoes do not turn green

Paprika potatoes (*for 4*)

1 onion	1 teaspoon paprika
1 tablespoon dripping	¼ pint (⅛l; ½ cup) stock
1lb (450g) potatoes	4 tablespoons yoghourt

Open a new packet of paprika for the occasion. There is nothing as fugitive as the sweet aroma of this spice. If you use an aged packet, even from an airtight tin, all those dedicated, Hungarian paprika-blenders, whose noses equal those of wine-tasters, have blended in vain. Fry the onion in the dripping until it is golden and transparent. Add the thickly sliced, thinly peeled potatoes and sprinkle with paprika. Add the stock, cover, and simmer for 1 hour, tightly covered. Before dishing up, cover with yoghourt (the health-food sort is best), just giving it time to heat up. Powder with more paprika and sprinkle with chopped chives. This can be a main dish – it is eaten as such all over the Balkans.

Potato pancakes

1lb (450g) creamy, mashed potato	1 clove of garlic, crushed
	salt
½ teaspoon thyme or marjoram	pepper
	1 egg, beaten
1oz (25g; ¼ cup) flour	½ pint (¼l; 1 cup) milk
1 onion, finely chopped	butter or oil

Mix all the ingredients together, finally binding with the egg and milk to make a batter. Cook little round cakes of this batter in butter or oil in a wide shallow pan. Crisp and brown the cakes on both sides; lovely with ham or bacon and apple sauce.

Potato dumplings (*for 6–8*)

These dumplings, beloved of the Swiss and the Bavarians, are eaten with onion sauce or simply with brown butter.

Grate 1lb (450g) of raw potatoes and plunge them at once into cold water to preserve the colour. Mash an equal quantity of cooked potatoes. Drain the watery mush, passing it through a cheesecloth as though you were making a jelly. Combine the two sorts of potato, add 1oz (25g; ¼ cup) of flour, seasoning (including a pinch of nutmeg), and finally bind the mass with an egg or two. Dice 3 slices of white bread, and fry in butter until golden. Draw off the heat. Form the potato dough into dumplings the size of a child's fist. Press a few of the bread cubes into each, and plunge into boiling stock or salted water. Cook for 15–20 minutes; to test if they are done, pierce with a skewer or knitting needle. If it comes out clean, fish out the dumplings. Serve as above or, as is often done in mountainous wooded regions, as an accompaniment to venison, roast boar or hare, all beautifully juicy and larded with bacon, and eaten with a sour-cream sauce and freshly picked cranberries.

Gratin Saint Hubert (*for 6*)

2lb (900g) potatoes	milk
4oz (110g; 1 cup) Gruyère or Bel Paese cheese	salt, pepper
	nutmeg
1 thick slice ham	butter
scant ¾ pint (½l; 1½ cups)	¼ pint (⅛l; ½ cup) cream

Peel the potatoes and grate them into a bowl of cold water. Grate the cheese and cut the ham into little strips. Butter an oval gratin dish. Take half the grated potato, squeeze it dry and put it in a layer in the bottom of the gratin dish. Put a layer of half the cheese over it, then the ham. Add the rest of the potatoes, squeezed dry, more cheese, and pour over the milk, well-seasoned with salt, pepper and nutmeg.

Cook in a moderately hot oven (Reg 5/375°F) for 1 hour, then pour the cream over the top and put under heat for 10 minutes, or until the cream is nicely browned. Originally this was served with a ring of little roast thrushes crowning it, but it is good without the sacrifice of so many songs.

Bauern Frühstück

Farmers' breakfast is the exact translation of the name of a stout potato pancake, which used to be the first meal of the day along the Baltic coast. It is no longer eaten first thing in the morning by anyone, but is still a good, if hefty, supper dish. Render some diced, rather fatty bacon in a shallow pan, and when the oily juices run freely, add as much diced cooked potato as will fill the pan. When everything is browned nicely throughout, stir in lightly beaten eggs, reckoning 1 egg per person. Sprinkle with chives, and eat with a green salad.

German Kartoffel-puffer

These Teutonic potato pancakes are made from raw grated potatoes. When done to perfection, they have succulent insides and crisp exteriors with lacy edges which are the best part. They can be eaten as a pudding – with puréed apple, which should be on the sour side, or stewed bilberries, or other stewed fruit with sugar – as a savoury, with lettuce, a green bean salad, or with chilled sour cream and sharp marinated herring.
The batter – 1 egg to each 1lb (450g) of potatoes, grated – is seasoned with a good pinch of salt and spooned into a well-greased shallow pan with a dessertspoon. The pancakes should be no larger than half of a man's hand, and as soon as you have established just how the mixture is going to spread, it is best to fry several spoonfuls at a time. Do not turn the pancakes before they are brown on the lower side, or they will disintegrate.

Heaven and earth

This is a Westphalian dish, best described as sweet and sour mashed potatoes. It is made of 1 apple – heaven – to every 5 medium-sized potatoes – earth. The peeled potatoes are boiled for 10 minutes, and are joined by the peeled apple(s).

When all is tender, drain, add a knob of butter, and mash up the contents of the pan. This is very nice with fried liver, bacon, or a combination of both.

Baked stuffed potatoes with cheese (*for 6*)

6 nice medium-sized unblemished potatoes of approximately similar size	1 egg
	salt
	cayenne pepper
	2oz (50g; ¼ cup) butter
12oz (335g; 3 cups) Cheddar cheese, grated	¼ pint (⅛l; ½ cup) creamy milk

Scrub the potatoes, prick them, roll them in salt and bake them for 1½ hours in a moderate oven (Reg 4/350°F), or for 1 hour in a fairly hot oven (Reg 6/400°F). Take out the potatoes, cut them in half lengthways and turn out the insides into a bowl, forking the pulp out lightly rather than scooping it out with a spoon. Keep the skins.

Bring the milk to the boil and pour it into the potato, whisking with a fork until you have a smooth purée, free from lumps. Beat in the egg, the cheese and the butter, and season with salt and cayenne pepper. Pile the mixture back into the potato skins, fork the tops nicely and bake in a moderate oven (Reg 4/350°F) for 15 minutes. Finish by browning under a flame.

Stuffings can of course be varied: the potato pulp, mixed with half its volume of chopped sautéed onion and flavoured with paprika, gives you potatoes *à la hongroise*; mixed with sausage meat, the dish is called *à la charcutière*; spinach and Mornay sauce make it florentine; tuna fish and garlic, *à la provençale*; thick cream and chives give a luscious mash; and there is one version, called *Maintenon*, in which a mixture of chicken breasts, truffles and mushrooms bound

in a Soubise sauce are used – but for this dish the potato itself is incidental.

JERUSALEM ARTICHOKE
Helianthus tuberosus

When this knobbly tuber first arrived in Europe from Nova Scotia in the seventeenth century, people took it for a rather unattractive potato. It is, however, nothing of the sort; nor is it an artichoke (although its taste is not dissimilar); nor does it have the remotest connection with Jerusalem. This name is thought to be a corruption of its Italian name, *Girasole*, the word for sunflower to which it is related.

Etymologists have lately pointed out that the English used the term 'Jerusalem artichoke' long before the Italians adopted their name for the tuber, and no new explanation has so far been offered.

In France, where it is known as *topinambour* after the Nova Scotian tribe of that name, whose visit to Paris coincided with the arrival of the Jerusalem artichoke, it has never quite made the grade in *haute cuisine*. It is delicious nevertheless, with nutrients similar to those of the potato, and of all vegetables it is the easiest to grow.

Basic treatment

The Jerusalem artichoke used to be a horror to scrape or peel, because of its knobbliness. Luckily the varieties now grown are infinitely smoother, and much easier to handle. Like potatoes, they are better cooked and skinned afterwards. If you are using them for soup and have to peel them beforehand, take care not to let them blacken: acidulated water will help them to keep their colour.

To bake artichokes – delicious with pork or veal – parboil them, then skin them, and arrange them round the joint in the roasting tin. To boil or steam, allow as much time as you would give potatoes. Use them in croquettes; eat them parboiled and fried; make fritters; bake them au gratin with a Mornay sauce; serve them cold, sliced or diced, in a Vinaigrette or thin mayonnaise as a salad. Best of all, use them in a very thick and filling soup.

Jerusalem artichokes Vinaigrette

This is a remarkable winter reminder of a summer salad made from the hearts of globe artichokes. Simply boil and skin the Jerusalem artichokes, and slice them into a shallow dish. Pour the Vinaigrette sauce over them while they are still tepid, and allow to cool.

Jerusalem artichoke soup (*for 4–6*)

1lb (450g) artichokes	2 egg yolks
1 small onion, chopped	6 tablespoons thick cream
butter	salt
1 pint (¾l; 2 cups) chicken stock	pepper
	parsley

Parboil, skin and dice the artichokes. Fry the onion in a heavy saucepan with butter until transparent. Add the artichokes, fry together for a few minutes, and then fill the pan with chicken stock and allow to bubble gently for about 30 minutes until the vegetables are done. Mash gently with a potato masher and simmer some more. Beat the cream into the egg yolks and put into the soup. Heat through until the soup thickens, and season. Serve with chopped parsley.

Go easy on the seasoning. As the artichokes have a very delicate flavour of their own, resist the temptation to throw in handfuls of herbs.

How to grow Jerusalem artichokes

There are white, reddish-skinned and purple varieties. Jerusalem artichokes will grow anywhere and everywhere – there is no less demanding, less fussy vegetable. They do best, however, in lightish soil. The tubers should be planted in spring 3in (8cm) deep, 16in (40cm) apart, leave 3ft (1m) between the drills. Apart from a little hoeing (if you are a perfectionist) and some watering in very dry weather, they need no further attention. They will grow, making a handsome tall screen. Properly sited, they make a good windbreak for other, more delicate subjects. The leaves should be cut down in the early winter, but the tubers may be left in the ground and lifted as required. Any forgotten Jerusalem artichokes, however, will spread and re-appear in the following year, so if you have other plans for the area, be sure to lift every last one before the growing season comes round again.

1. Jerusalem artichokes can be grown in any odd corner

2. They will put up with neglect but repay watering

3. New tubers form around the root of the parent plant

4. After the greenery is cut down, tubers can be left in the ground until wanted

PODS

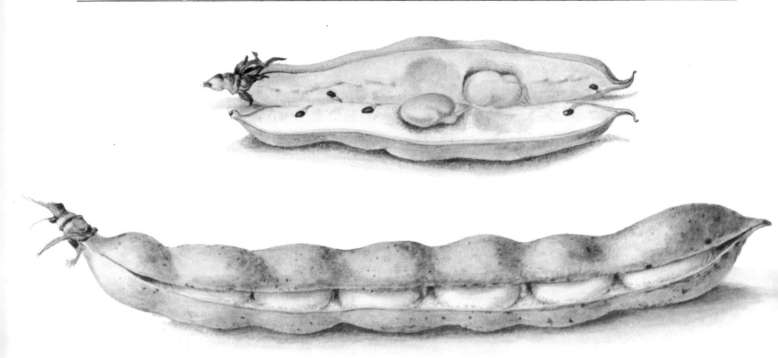

Broad bean *Vicia fabia*

Most members of the bean family come from South America, although some came to Western Europe with the Romans. The broad bean, for instance, is one of the most ancient of our vegetables, and originated in the East. All beans are rich in protein and have been regarded as a valuable food since time immemorial. Lima beans, to which the broad bean is the closest equivalent, are to Brazil what potatoes are to Ireland. They used to be interplanted with corn, and were said to keep down weeds. French explorers are credited with introducing them to the Old World. (The Lima variety did not do well in European weather conditions, but green beans flourished and became known, in due course, as French beans.) Culpeper's *Herbal* says that they belong to the goddess Venus, and recommends them to lovers.

BROAD BEANS *Vicia fabia*

This vegetable is at its best when it is very, very young. As it is impossible to buy in this state, it can only be properly enjoyed when it is home grown. Another reason for cultivating broad beans is that a row or two make the vegetable plot look hopeful very soon after the seeds have gone in. They are quick to germinate, and even the primary leaves look stout, unwhiskery, and full of promise.

Basic treatment

Very young and tender broad beans can be cooked complete with pod, but in the main, they should be shelled and cooked in boiling salted water for 5–15 minutes (depending on their freshness; broad beans become hard and mealy if they are cooked too long). Older broad beans can be slipped out of their individual tough skins after blanching, then cooked in a very little boiling water for a few minutes. To steam, sprinkle generously with salt and put the beans in a steamer over boiling water. Cover, and cook for 10–15 minutes.

Tiny, shelled raw broad beans, which are, incidentally, very rich in pantothenic acid, a vitamin of the B group which is necessary for the health of the skin, are a delicious hors d'oeuvre served with a homemade mayonnaise or Vinaigrette dressing. Young beans, in or out of their pods, are good just tossed in butter and sprinkled with chopped summer savory or parsley. More mature broad beans can be dished up with white sauce, onion sauce, chopped ham or bacon, or with rings of fried onion, or they can be cooked with a bacon bone, chicken carcass, or garlic; and very old ones, with eyes that have turned black, can be used as a purée.

Broad bean soup (*for 4*)

Blanch 1lb (450g) of mature, shelled broad beans for 10 minutes in just enough boiling salted water to barely cover them. Keep the water and skin the beans. Fry a little chopped onion in butter, then add the beans. Cover the pan and let the onion and the beans cook until they are tender. Mash or sieve the vegetables and return them to a clean saucepan. Add 1 pint ($\frac{3}{4}$l; 2 cups) of milk or stock, or $\frac{1}{2}$ pint ($\frac{1}{4}$l; 1 cup) of each, and the bean water, and reheat very slowly. Season with salt, pepper and a little sugar, and just before serving thicken the soup with an egg yolk beaten into thick cream.

Broad bean purée

An excellent way of using beans which have survived to old age. Cook 1lb (450g) of shelled beans together with 3 or 4 artichoke bottoms, the heart of a lettuce, a handful of peas and 1 small onion. When everything is tender, slip the beans out of their skins and put all the vegetables through a sieve, then return the purée to a clean pan and stir vigorously until it starts to thicken. Add little pieces of butter and season with salt and pepper as you stir. Add 2 tablespoons of thick cream just before serving. Delicious with boiled ham.

Raw broad bean salad

Shell 1lb (450g) of tiny, new broad beans and roughly dice half a cucumber. Mix them together with a sprinkling of fresh herbs and a finely chopped, hard-boiled egg. Serve with French dressing.

Broad beans with pork (*for 4*)

1 thick slice belly pork or fat bacon	2 cloves of garlic, crushed
olive oil	fresh coriander, chopped
2 large onions, sliced	2 teaspoons ground cummin
8 thick slices black pudding	salt
3lb (1·35kg) broad beans, shelled	pepper
	sugar
	$\frac{1}{2}$ pint ($\frac{1}{4}$l; 1 cup) stock

Fry the chopped-up pork in the oil in a heavy casserole until browned. Add the onions and cook until they become transparent. Now put in the slices of black pudding and fry, stirring all the time to prevent it sticking. Add all the other ingredients and cook, covered, in a medium oven, for about 30 minutes.

GREEN BEANS *Phaseolus vulgaris*

Green beans come in great variety. Some are glossy, some velvety. Some are mottled, and some are not green at all, but purple, changing colour only as they come in contact with boiling water. It is worth while looking for some of the less usual varieties for decorative purposes as well as culinary ones: purple, red, white and particoloured blossoms are a noble sight. In fact, beans used to be grown by the Victorians chiefly for their ornamental appearance, and for the delicious scent of their flowers. But people soon realized what the Ancients had always known, that beans, whatever their colour, provide more nourishment per square inch of soil.

How to grow broad beans

Broad beans will grow well in all types of soil, but it must be well manured a month before planting. For best results, sow in early spring in well-dug, rich, finely raked soil. Choose a day when the weather is suitable – never sow in damp or frozen conditions – and sow again in succession until early summer. Sow in staggered rows by making holes with a small stick and dropping the seeds in snugly. They can also be sown in early winter for early crops, or in midwinter under cloches or in polythene tunnels, this protection being removed in spring when the plants are at the top of the cloche. The rows are kept hoed, and any sign of blackfly should be tackled at once with a spray. The flowering top should be pinched out when the plants are in full bloom.

Dwarf varieties, good for small gardens, give you a lot of beans and take up little room, and the flowers look as decorative and exotic – white, pale purple or multi-coloured – as they smell sweet.

1. Sow seeds with the scar downwards 8in (20cm) apart

2. Stagger them in double rows 24in (60cm) apart, and hoe regularly

3. Rows of string support the plants which are inclined to be floppy

4. Pinch out the tops where blackfly like to cluster

Basic treatment

All varieties of green bean should be washed and topped and tailed. The young ones can be left whole, but you should remove the strings from the sides of older beans before slicing them obliquely into thin strips. Snap beans or Bobi beans should be cut straight across. Cook in boiling salted water for 5–10 minutes. Timing depends on the age of the bean and the thickness of the slice, and is very critical. Beans are almost as unpleasant undercooked as they are when overcooked. Like pasta they should be *al dente* – resilient but not over-chewy. Green beans should be very green. To improve the colour, cook them in an uncovered pan and add the salt only at the last minute.

Cooked beans can be tossed in butter and sprinkled with herbs – summer savory is one of the best – and served with garlic or anchovy butter.

French beans and bacon

Chop up a rasher of lean bacon or a small piece of ham, and fry. Add sliced, cooked green beans and some shreds of skinned tomato flesh, and shake the pan over the heat. You can elevate this dish to a main course by serving it with rounds or fingers of fried bread, sprinkled with grated cheese and browned in the oven; or with *Diablotins*, which are round thin slices of French bread covered with thick Béchamel sauce, sprinkled with grated Parmesan cheese, and browned.

Greek beans

Break smallish green beans in halves and cook them in salted water. Drain them well. Put into a saucepan ¼ pint (⅛l; 1 cup) of stock, parsley, 1 or 2 onions finely chopped, and celery or celeriac cut into thin strips (or a seasoning of celery salt). Bring to the boil, add the beans, cook until the onion is soft, and thicken the sauce with 2 egg yolks beaten with the juice of half a lemon. Serve with pieces of fried bread.

French beans with cheese

Drain some cooked beans and put them into a greased fire-proof dish. Add ¼ pint (1 cup) of grated cheese, 1 level tablespoon of melted butter, and ⅛ pint (30ml; ½ cup) thin white sauce or milk. Finish in the oven, sprinkle with more cheese and brown quickly before serving.

German runner beans

Blanch some sliced beans in boiling salted water for about 5 minutes. Meanwhile, fry half a sliced onion in butter until transparent. Take the pan off the heat and add enough flour to make a smooth white sauce with the water from the beans. Add the beans and simmer until they have finished cooking.

French beans in salads

Whole cooked French beans are a delicious salad ingredient. They should be seasoned with salt, pepper, olive oil and lemon juice while they are still warm, and then left to cool. Mix them with either sliced hard-boiled egg, black olives, blanched flowerets of cauliflower, other cooked cold vegetables, or thin slices of raw mushroom and cucumber, or serve them on their own. As beans are fairly substantial, any of the above salads would be an ideal first course, or a vegetable course in its own right.

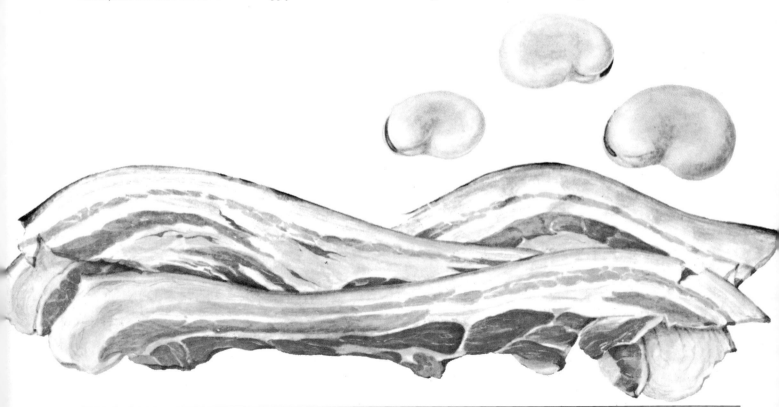

Bean and potato omelette

Proceed as for German runner beans, then add to the beans an equal quantity of cooked and mashed potato. Flatten out the mixture with a spatula and pour over 1 egg which has been beaten up with a little milk, salt and pepper, and fry, until the egg mixture is golden, turning once. Sprinkle with cheese and serve at once.

Salade niçoise

In a salad bowl, mix equal parts of cooked, diced green beans and cooked diced potatoes, in a French dressing. Decorate with anchovies and black olives, and surround with wedges of raw tomato.

For a more substantial *salade niçoise*, you can add tinned (drained) tuna fish, capers, and quartered hard-boiled eggs, and it will still be true to its name, but it is on the green beans that it depends.

French bean and prawn hors d'oeuvre

Dress the cooked beans, cut into convenient lengths, with oil and lemon while they are warm. Pile them on a dish, making a crater at the top. Fill this with boiled prawns mixed in mayonnaise, and sprinkled with chives. Serve with crusty French bread, warmed in the oven.

Beans in sour cream (*for 4 as a first course; for 6 as a vegetable served with roasts or poultry*)

Cook 1lb (450g) of runner beans, and drain them well. Season 4 tablespoons sour cream with salt, pepper, nutmeg and caraway seeds. Pour the cream over the beans and mix well. Put the beans into a buttered, shallow fireproof dish and top with a handful of breadcrumbs tossed in browned butter. Bake in a medium oven until brown and crisp on top, and serve immediately.

Tuscan beans (*for 4*)

The sauce for this dish should be light and fluffy, of the consistency of whipped mayonnaise. It is good served with fish.
Slice and cook 1lb (450g) of French or runner beans, drain and put them on one side to keep warm. Put into a mixing bowl 2 small egg yolks, 2 tablespoons of white grape juice or dry white wine sweetened with 1 teaspoon of castor sugar, and 1 tablespoon of white wine vinegar, and whisk these ingredients together over a pan of boiling water until the sauce thickens and begins to froth. Pour over the beans and serve immediately.

French beans and almonds

Almonds were once used as a condiment, as salt and pepper are today. Their crunchiness, added to beans that still have some bite, is used to great advantage in this dish. Cook some small French beans, and while they are cooking, lightly brown the flaked almonds in very little butter, shaking the pan constantly. Be careful, the almonds will turn dark brown very quickly. Season, and add the almonds to the drained beans. This dish makes a vegetable course on its own, in the French manner, or as an accompaniment to veal.

Sauces for beans

To ring the changes with fully matured beans, partly cook them in the usual way, then stew in butter until tender. Moisten with a spoonful or two of either thick brown gravy, tomato sauce, cheese sauce, or thick cream; or fry them gently in a little olive oil with a bit of garlic.

How to grow runner beans
Runners, climbing French and dwarf French beans all like deeply dug, well-manured soil and a different site each year. Climbing beans need a strong framework, this can be a screen of 8ft (2·5m) bamboo or bean poles, or a frame of poles with strings running down and secured by skewers or wire, or a tripod of poles tied securely at the top. A narrow site by a wall is also good, as they can climb up strings attached to the wall and look decorative, or make a temporary screen anywhere in the garden. They can also be grown in window boxes, in rich soil, making a green curtain by the window. Runner beans are sown from late spring to midsummer, and thinned if necessary to 12in (30cm) apart. Plenty of water is needed, and a spraying with water at flowering time helps the beans to set. When they have climbed to 7–8ft (2–2·5m), pinch out the tops. Pick the beans regularly and early – the smaller they are, the more delicious they taste.

1. Sow beans on a different site each year   *2. Water them well; they will climb up their poles*

PEAS *Pisum sativum*

Peas were well known even to the earliest Europeans. 'Runcible peas', large, mealy and not very sweet, clambered about in early English cottage gardens. They were largely used to make 'pottage', a healthful thick soup, but are also known to have been served with spit-roast whale in the sixteenth century at a Lord Mayor's banquet. The 'sugar pea', a sweeter variety, arrived on the scene during the seventeenth century. Enormously expensive, these peas became a status symbol. Dutch King William III made himself even more unpopular with his unwilling English subjects by absentmindedly eating the entire dishful proffered at the royal table; and in France, according to

Mme de Sévigné, the Court talked of nothing but green peas and 'the impatience to eat them, the pleasure of eating them and the desire soon to eat them again.' Louis XIV's *fermier-général*, anxious to impress a lovely lady who was on a diet, invited her to take a dish of milk at his house – and went so far as to feed a cow exclusively on tiny peas for two days prior to her visit. Madame loved the milk; just as well, since the cow had been eating the equivalent of green caviar.

The size of a pea is not invariably related to its age, but to its variety. The sort that comes in tins called *petits pois*, for instance, is full grown, very sweet, and can be allowed to mature in the garden, although if left too long on the vine, it can be as bullet-like as an overgrown giant. The *mange-tout* pea, as its name suggests, is eaten pod and all. It should be used as soon as possible after picking, and it too should be picked young. With age it develops strings, and needs to be dethreaded like a bean.

Peas are richer in proteins and carbohydrates than most vegetables, and contain vitamins A, B and C. Unfortunately, they are in the top range for calories – about 90 to a helping.

Basic treatment

Peas, whether podded or cooked in their shells, will go hard if left on the boil too long. According to age, size and freshness, they will take anything from 5–15 minutes.

The first pick of the crop will have a delicate flavour which it would be a shame to mask – so the rule is *no* mint, *no* parsley – just a little water, a pinch of salt, and some fresh butter when they are done. Older peas can be cooked in stock, with onions and lettuce, with ham, with mint and a sprinkling of sugar; their pods can make stock for soup.

Green pea soup

Peel 4 large floury potatoes, chop 2 onions, and boil in plenty of salted water, together with 1lb (450g) of shelled green peas. Giants will do very well – in fact, better than really tiny *petits pois*, which are not mealy enough and which it would in any case be a pity to mash or mouli. When all the vegetables are soft, they then go back into the pan with as much of their stock as will produce a thin purée-like consistency, and are allowed to simmer for about 10 minutes before they are drawn off the heat and bound with a well-beaten mixture of 4 tablespoons of cream and 2 egg yolks. As a finishing touch, add a walnut of butter, cut into tiny pieces. Some people like to garnish this soup with minute cubes of fried bread or ham, but it is very good on its own.

Petits pois à la française

Line a small saucepan with the outer leaves of a lettuce; add some shelled peas, a peeled silver-skinned onion, a knob of butter, a lump of sugar, a pinch of salt, and a good tablespoon of water. Cover the contents of the pan with a large lettuce leaf. Cook gently, lifting the lettuce lid – which will collapse during the cooking process – to test for tenderness. It is customary but not strictly necessary to remove the lettuce before dishing up.

Rice and pea pudding

2oz (50g; $\frac{1}{4}$ cup) butter	chopped
$\frac{1}{2}$lb (225g; $1\frac{1}{4}$ cups) Italian risotto rice	$\frac{1}{2}$lb (225g; $2\frac{3}{4}$ cups) peas, cooked
$\frac{1}{2}$ pint ($\frac{1}{4}$l; 1 cup) beef stock	4 eggs, beaten
2 onions, sliced	salt
$\frac{1}{4}$lb (110g; $\frac{3}{4}$ cup) ham,	pepper

Melt half the butter and fry the rice gently until each piece is coated, add the stock and cover the pan. Simmer the rice until it is cooked – about 15–20 minutes – adding more stock if the rice sticks to the pan. Meanwhile, cook the onions in the remaining butter, and add them and the chopped ham to the rice when it has about 10 minutes of cooking time left. When the rice is done, add the cooked peas and the eggs, and season to taste. Transfer the mixture to a well-buttered fireproof dish and cook in a hot oven until the eggs set, about 10–15 minutes.

Italian green pea pudding

This dish is a cross between a soufflé and a traditional

How to grow peas

There are peas to mature early, second early, or main crop; they come in two types, round and wrinkled. The round seeds are hardier and may be sown early, but the wrinkled seeds give you sweeter peas. All peas need soil which was well manured the previous winter. They should be sown in drills in succession from early spring in short rows and at roughly 3-week intervals to the late summer. As the plants emerge they are open to attack from birds, so protect them with bent-wire peaguards. As soon as possible give them support, like twiggy sticks, to prevent collapse. To use the space to the best advantage, you can intercrop peas with quick-growing things like radish or lettuce. The early pea varieties sown in spring should be ready to eat in 11–12 weeks; second earlies in 12–13 weeks; and the main crop in 13–14 weeks. Water well, mulch to retain the moisture and be sure to pick regularly – the more you pick, the more each plant will produce.

1. Spring: sow 2–3in (5–8cm) deep, at the same distance apart as the given height of the plant

2. Water, hoe and mulch, and support with twiggy sticks or wire netting

Peas *Pisum sativum*

English pease pudding. It is a good way of using up the last of the crop, and the recipe is suitable for any green vegetable that is past its prime.

Soften a small, chopped onion in butter until transparent. Add 2lb (900g) of shelled peas and cover with water; add a pinch of salt and simmer gently until tender.

Meanwhile make a thick Béchamel sauce using a good knob of butter, 1 tablespoon of flour and 4 tablespoons of warmed milk. Season and add 2 tablespoons of chopped ham and 1 tablespoon of grated Parmesan cheese.

Drain the peas and put all but a small handful through a sieve. Return the purée to a clean pan, and add the Béchamel sauce, a bit of butter and the whole peas. Mix and allow to cool. Separate 3 eggs and stir the yolks into the purée, then fold in the beaten whites. Pour into a buttered soufflé dish and steam for about 1 hour in a covered pan. To serve, turn the pudding out on to a dish.

Petits pois en bouillabaisse

1 onion	bouquet of bay, thyme,
3 tablespoons olive oil	fennel and parsley
5–6 large new potatoes (the	salt, pepper
waxy ones if possible)	pinch of saffron
2lb (900g) shelled peas	6 eggs
3 cloves of garlic	6 slices French bread

Chop an onion and let it soften gently in the olive oil, without browning. Add the potatoes, scraped and cut into slices about $\frac{1}{2}$in (1·5cm) thick. Stir them around for a minute or two without letting them brown, then add $1\frac{3}{4}$ pints (1l; $3\frac{1}{4}$ cup) of boiling water and throw in the peas. Add the crushed cloves of garlic and the bouquet of herbs. Season with salt, pepper and a large pinch of saffron. Cover the pan and let the mixture simmer slowly.

When the potatoes are tender and the peas cooked, take 1 egg for each person and carefully break the eggs into the pan one at a time, so that they poach in the gently bubbling liquid for about 3–4 minutes.

To serve this dish, put a slice of bread in each soup plate and carefully spoon over it an egg and some soup.

Risi e bisi

1oz (25g; $\frac{1}{8}$ cup) butter	up to 2 pints ($1\frac{1}{4}$l; 4 cups)
2–3 tablespoons olive oil	light stock
6 spring onions	1lb (450g) shelled peas
12oz (335g; 2 cups) Italian	salt, pepper
rice	a little extra butter
4 tablespoons chopped ham	2–3 tablespoons grated
(optional)	Parmesan cheese

Melt the butter and oil in a heavy saucepan and cook the onions until transparent. Add the rice and stir it round until it glistens. Add the ham, and pour on 1 pint ($\frac{3}{4}$l; 2 cups) of stock. When it has bubbled up, throw in the peas. Let it cook steadily for 25–30 minutes, until the rice is tender and all the stock absorbed, adding a little more if it becomes too dry.

Just before serving, taste for seasoning and stir in the cream, a little fresh butter and half the Parmesan cheese. Hand the remaining grated cheese separately.

Stewed peas with ham

Melt a good lump of lard and an equivalent amount of butter in a heavy saucepan, and gently fry a sliced onion until golden but not brown. Remove the pan from the heat and add 3 tablespoons of chicken stock, 1 teaspoon of chopped parsley, 4 heaped tablespoons of chopped ham, and salt and pepper. Return the pan to the heat and when the stock is boiling add 1lb (450g) of shelled peas. Cover the pan with a tightly fitting lid and cook slowly until the peas are tender. Serve with croûtons, as a course on its own.

PULSE

Dried peas, beans and their kin have been with us from the beginning of time. Mounds of them have been found in ancient burial chambers from Egypt to Peru, to sustain the dear departed on their passage to the great beyond. The Bible refers to them more than once. The mess of pottage for which Esau sold his birthright was made of lentils; and the Children of Israel were exhorted on their Exodus to carry beans and lentils – high in protein – 'to make bread thereof'. As for Western fairy tales the princess who spent an uncomfortable night on a bed piled high with mattresses, getting up black and blue in the morning, had her sensibilities outraged by a chick pea; and Grimm's Cinderella, poor thing, was given the boring task of sorting the dud ones from an entire sackful.

Basic treatment

All pulse need to be carefully picked over. Failing the assistance of Cinderella's pigeons, the easiest way is to place them in a large bowl of cold water, and wait for the hollow ones to rise to the top. (Small stones, etc, will still need to be picked out by hand.) Then rinse well, and soak for not less than 2 and not more than 10 hours – any longer and they may start to ferment. To cook them, drain, and put in a saucepan with fresh water. They will absorb a lot of water as

they swell up, so have at least 2 fingers' depth of clear water above the vegetable line. Simmering times: about 2–2½ hours for beans, and about 1–2 hours for peas and lentils; but much depends on how long they have soaked.

Minestrone

Eaten with grated Parmesan cheese, which is served separately, minestrone can be made with whatever vegetables are at hand, but haricot beans and stock are its *sine qua non*.

Simmer 2 tablespoons soaked haricot beans in about 1 pint (¾l; 2 cups) of stock for about 30 minutes. Meanwhile dice, slice, shred and crush 2 carrots, 2 tomatoes, 2 onions, 2 sticks celery, a quarter of a white cabbage and/or whatever else is to hand, and 1 clove of garlic.

Gently sweat this vegetable mixture in oil to release the flavours, add 2 further pints (1¼l; 4 cups) of stock, stirring well to loosen any vegetables that may cling to the bottom of the pan. Bring to the boil, add the beans together with their liquid, and simmer until all the vegetables are cooked.

Arter med fläsk (*for 6–8*)

In Sweden this is eaten every Thursday, even though King Eric XIV died on a Thursday in 1577 after his brother had slipped poison into his yellow pea soup. It is very delicious and any that is left over can be reheated the next day.

1lb (450g) yellow split peas	2 teaspoons dried marjoram
5 pints (3·75l; 10 cups)	and 1 teaspoon dried
water	ginger *or* a good pinch of
1lb (450g) piece streaky	thyme
bacon or bacon hock	salt
3 onions	freshly ground black pepper

Put the split peas in a large pan with the water. Bring slowly to the boil and cook for 1 hour before adding the piece of bacon, the onions, marjoram and ginger (or thyme). Continue cooking, covered, over a moderate heat until the bacon is done – about a further 1½ hours – adding more water as required and seasoning with salt and pepper, if necessary. You can now take out the bacon and serve the soup as it is, or sieve it together with the onions for a finer soup.

Pasta e fagioli (*for 6*)

4oz (110g; ½ cup) dried	1–2 onions
haricot beans or, better,	2–3 cloves of garlic
the slightly larger	2–3 sticks of celery
pink-speckled pale beige	3 tablespoons olive oil
pinto beans	thyme
5 pints (3·75l; 10 cups	4oz (110g; 1 cup) short
water or stock	macaroni or ditali
1 small bacon hock or a	parsley
lump of salt pork	grated Parmesan cheese

Soak the beans and the bacon or salt pork overnight.
Strain and put in a large pan with 5 pints (3·75l; 10

cups) fresh water and bring slowly to the boil. Do not add salt. Simmer until the beans are very well cooked. Remove the hock or salt pork, skin it and cut it into cubes.

Chop the onion, garlic and celery. Heat the olive oil in a large saucepan and fry the bacon or pork, onions, garlic and celery. When they start to brown and give off an appetizing smell, pour in the beans and their cooking liquid. Add more liquid at this point if necessary.

Let the soup come to the boil. Skim off any froth that rises to the top. Add the thyme, and salt if needed, and let it cook for 20 minutes. Now add the pasta and let the soup boil steadily until this is tender.

Sprinkle on a generous amount of chopped parsley, and plenty of grated Parmesan cheese. Serve with more cheese. You can use red kidney beans for this soup if you like them better.

In Italy, *Pasta e fagioli* is such a well-loved soup that it is eaten with pleasure throughout the year. If the weather is too sweltering for it to be eaten hot, then it is eaten cold.

Potage Saint-Germain (*for 4*)

1lb (450g) dried peas	1 leek, diced
water or stock to cover	½ pint (¼l; 1 cup) stock,
1 large onion, diced	heated
1 large carrot, diced	salt, pepper

Drain the soaked peas and immerse them in water (or stock). Add the peeled, diced vegetables and simmer until tender – about 1 hour. Press through a sieve, thinning the mixture down with the heated stock to the required consistency of thin cream. Season and serve with tiny croûtons.

Three-bean salad (*for 4–6*)

4oz (110g; ½ cup) red	*for the dressing:*
kidney beans	8 tablespoons olive oil
4oz (110g; ½ cup) haricot	1 tablespoon wine vinegar
beans or flageolets	salt
4oz (110g; ½ cup) chick	chilli (about as much as you
peas	would normally use of
6 spring onions, chopped	pepper)
bunch of parsley, chopped	

Soak the beans and the chick peas overnight, in separate bowls. Cook, drain and cool the beans and chick peas, separately.

Combine them in a bowl. Make a dressing of the olive oil, wine vinegar, salt and chilli. Toss the beans thoroughly in the dressing.

Allow the salad to stand in the dressing for 1–2 hours. Add the chopped onions just before serving and finally sprinkle with chopped parsley. The combination of the beans, rich red and pearly white or soft pale green, and the chick peas, a warm biscuit colour, is very beautiful; and the salad, although rather filling, tastes extremely good.

Brown bean salad

Soak 4oz (110g; $\frac{1}{2}$ cup) brown Italian beans, and simmer them with a bay leaf in freshly salted water for 2 hours or until they are tender. Let them cool in their liquor. Cook a peeled onion in water until soft, and chop. Skin 2 tomatoes, slice and cut crosswise. Drain the beans, fish out the bay leaf, and mix together with the tomatoes and onion in a garlicky Vinaigrette.

Haricot beans

Take, white, green, red, brown or black, large or small – 3oz (75g; $\frac{1}{4}$ cup) – beans per person; water; bouquet of parsley, thyme, bay leaf, celery stalk, and garlic if liked; salt.

Put the beans in a saucepan with cold water. Add no salt but put in the herbs and garlic (and a piece of salt pork or bacon if you like). Bring slowly to the boil and cook gently for about 1 hour or until the beans are tender. Add salt about 15 minutes before draining the beans. (Most of the liquid will have been absorbed.) Serve them as they are with plenty of freshly chopped parsley and butter; or bathed in a sauce of tomatoes and onion cooked in oil with a cupful of their own liquid; or stirred into a creamy sauce made with butter, flour and what is left of their own liquid, plus plenty of chopped parsley; or leave out the parsley and add chopped boiled bacon or ham.

Cold haricot beans make very good salads with Vinaigrette dressing and raw onion, tuna fish, green beans or just parsley.

Lentil purée

Soak 1lb (450g) of lentils, drain and rinse and bring them to the boil with 1 carrot, 1 onion, 1 bay leaf and 1 clove of garlic in about 1$\frac{1}{2}$ pints (about 1l; 3 cups) of salted water. Cooking time can be anything from 1–2 hours, depending on the sort of lentils you use. Stir them about occasionally, to check that they have not stuck to the bottom of the pan. Then drain and mouli them to a purée; this goes well with any sort of game.

Pease-pudding

The traditional way of preparing this dish is to soak and cook split peas for about 1 hour or until they are tender, and to pass them through a sieve. Into 1lb (450g) of this mash, stir 2 tablespoons of butter and 1 beaten egg. Beat well and tie loosely in a floured pudding cloth. Simmer for 1 hour and dish up. This is a classic accompaniment to pickled pork, and very good it is.

Curried eggs with dhal (for 4–6)

1lb (450g; 2$\frac{1}{3}$ cups) dhal	2 tablespoons curry powder
2 medium-sized onions	1 or 2 eggs for each person
2 tablespoons butter	salt

Dhal – the little yellow or orange or pink lentils – is such an easy thing to prepare, so delicious to eat and so relatively cheap, that it should become part of every good cook's repertoire. Ideally it is soft and somewhat liquid in texture, and the cheap lentils, so difficult to make appetizing in the ordinary way, make a thickish stew of exactly the right consistency in a very short time.

Soak them for 1–2 hours before cooking. Then simply fry the finely chopped onions in the butter without browning, stir in the curry powder and let it cook for a minute or two, then add the soaked, drained dhal. Stir it round, pour over enough water to cover by 1in (2·5cm) and simmer for about 30 minutes, adding more water if necessary. Towards the end of the cooking add salt.

Boil the eggs so that they are not too hard – about 8–9 minutes – shell and halve them and put them on top of the dhal on each person's plate. Serve with rice, if liked, and with mango chutney or lime pickle.

Dhal with chilli

4oz (110g; $\frac{1}{2}$ cup) dhal	3 cloves of garlic
1 pint ($\frac{3}{4}$l; 2 cups) water	1 green chilli
or stock	$\frac{1}{4}$ teaspoon chilli powder
pinch salt	$\frac{1}{4}$ teaspoon cummin seeds
$\frac{1}{4}$ teaspoon turmeric	1–2 tablespoons oil or
1 onion	melted butter

Pick over the dhal, wash it in several waters to free it of dust and starch. Put it in a pan with water, or stock if you have it, a pinch of salt and the turmeric.

Cook until tender – the cooking time varies according to how you like it (dry like rice or smooth and moist), and on the type of dhal you are cooking. When it is almost cooked, slice the onion and cloves of garlic and fry them in the oil or butter together with the sliced chilli, chilli powder and cummin seeds. When the onion is golden brown, add the dhal and some chopped green coriander if you have it. Cook, stirring, over a low heat for 5 minutes.

This reheats very well. If it becomes too dry add a little water or chicken stock. Serve it with curry; it is a practically indispensable accompaniment.

Boston baked beans (for 6–8)

1lb (450g) haricot beans	2 large tablespoons brown
1$\frac{1}{2}$lb (675g) collar of bacon	sugar
in a piece	salt, pepper
1 onion, stuck with 3 cloves	1 small tin tomatoes or 6
1 large tablespoon vinegar	medium-sized fresh
2 teaspoons mustard	tomatoes

Soak the beans overnight and soak the bacon separately. The next day drain the beans and put them in a large pan, well covered with cold water. Add 1 onion, stuck with 3 cloves, and simmer until the beans are just tender but not bursting.

Meanwhile, cut the bacon into 4 thick slices, and roast in a fairly hot oven (Reg 6/400°F) for 30 minutes. Drain most of the liquid from the beans (keeping it aside), season them with vinegar, mustard, sugar, salt and pepper. Cut up the boiled onion and put it with the beans.

Cut the rinds off the bacon and lay them in the bottom of a casserole. Thoroughly mix the beans, bacon and chopped tomatoes (skin them first if you are using fresh tomatoes); add the fat from the bacon and put the whole into the casserole.

Cook, well covered, at Reg 3/325°F for 2½–3 hours or even longer, adding some of the cooking liquid from the beans if it becomes too dry. The beans should be smoky from the bacon and very fragrant. They have a milder flavour than beans cooked with black treacle.

Cassoulet (*for 6*)

This is one of the great regional French dishes, invariably based on haricot beans, but containing a great mixture of meats: fresh or preserved goose, mutton, a hock of bacon, fresh belly pork and garlicky country sausage. The meats vary from district to district, but the system is always the same: they are prepared separately and put, together with their juices, between layers of pre-cooked beans in a great earthenware pot. The top layer of beans is always sealed with fresh breadcrumbs, and the whole goes into the oven for a final session, emerging as the richest imaginable dish.

Even without the smoked goose, or indeed without any goose at all, a very respectable *cassoulet* can be produced.

1½lb (675g) haricot beans	1lb (450g) breast of lamb
1 bouquet garni	lard, or goose or duck
2 carrots	dripping
2 onions, stuck with cloves	4 onions, chopped
1 small hock bacon or	4 cloves of garlic
bacon bone	a chunk of garlic sausage
1 small duck (or leftovers)	white breadcrumbs

Cover the beans in plenty of water, together with the herbs, the carrots, the clove-onions and the bacon, and cook until they are tender. Roast the duck, and as soon as it has yielded some dripping, cut up the breast of lamb, which should be browned in a shallow pan in dripping from the duck. Then add and brown the chopped onions and the garlic. Moisten with liquid ladled from the bean pan, cover and simmer for 2 hours or until tender. Keep warm. When the beans are soft, drain them, saving the liquid. Remove the bouquet garni, the hock of bacon and the clove-onions. Add the juices from the duck and the lamb. Thickly slice the sausage and the meats. Then, in an earthenware pot, make a layer of beans, reserving a quantity for your final layer. Make layers of the different meats, alternating with the beans, and finishing up with a top layer of beans. Cover with the breadcrumbs, dot with lard or dripping, and cook in a slow oven for 1 hour, adding a little of the bean liquid occasionally, to keep the cassoulet moist. Do not decant the cassoulet, but serve it straight from the oven.

Lamb and haricot beans

1½lb (675g) haricot beans	parsley
2 onions	1 pint (¾l; 2 cups) water
3 tablespoons cooking oil	or stock
2½lb (1¼kg) scrag or middle	salt, pepper
neck of lamb	2 cloves of garlic, sliced
3 tablespoons tomato puree	finely
bay leaf	

Cook the haricot beans slowly for 1 hour or until soft. Slice the onions and cook them gently in the oil. Take them out when soft and transparent and put in a fireproof dish. Now brown the lamb in the remaining oil and add it to the onions. Add all the remaining ingredients plus the drained, cooked beans. Cook in a moderate oven (Reg 4/350°F) for 2½ hours.

LEAVES

Spinach *Spinacia oleracea*

Many of the wild leafy plants, most of them rightly considered as weeds owing to their ability to turn up in the wrong places, taste good, and are good for you. All are best when they are young and fresh, and consequently most of them come into their own in the spring. They used to be welcomed as efficacious clearers of the blood after the winter, and used mostly in their raw state.

SPINACH *Spinacia oleracea*

In Renaissance times when spectacularly coloured food was admired, the deep green juice of spinach was used for 'marbling' paler dishes. Considered more a herb, spinach was not very successful as a vegetable. 'I know not for what it is good save to fill the belly,' moodily comments a sixteenth-century author, and seventeenth-century cooks were still hard put to it to find ways of making it acceptable. They par-boiled and chopped spinach, mixed it with eggs and bread-crumbs, salt and sugar, and made fritters to be eaten with sugar. Boiled soft, it was 'served forth' with currants, butter

and sugar. When it was baked, pre-cooked and chopped, and mixed with walnuts, oregano, currants, cinnamon, ginger, nutmeg and salt, butter, vinegar and sugar, the resulting dish was known as Florendine.

It was Popeye the Sailorman – the bristly cartoon hero of the 1920's – who did for spinach what no chef had hitherto managed to achieve. At the climax of each film, when he or his companion Olive Oyl were all but lost, the hero would nonchalantly open a tin of spinach, gain amazing strength, and save the situation. Children all over the world, deaf until then to the litany of 'spinach is good for you', got the message – and it is ironic that research now tells us that spinach does contain a substance, oxalate, which can be harmful if too much is eaten.

Basic treatment

Wash spinach several times in cold water, and when it is clean, put it in the saucepan with no extra water. The moisture that clings to the leaves is quite sufficient to prevent it from burning as you bring it *gently* to the boil. Stir until all the spinach has collapsed, then go on simmering it for 10 minutes or so. As for quantities; as it cooks, spinach decreases spectacularly in volume to about a quarter of what you started off with. When it is chopped, it looks even less.

Spinach is either chopped finely or served *en branche*. Nutmeg and cream are often added to spinach purée, but butter, as much as it can absorb, is what it chiefly needs. This also applies to non-chopped spinach.

Spinach soup (*for 4–6*)

1lb (450g) spinach	juice of $\frac{1}{2}$ large lemon
1 small onion or shallot	3 egg yolks
$1\frac{1}{2}$ pints (1l; 3 cups) chicken stock or stock cube in water	seasoning butter

Wash the spinach, clean and chop the onion or shallot finely. Melt the butter and sweat the onion very gently until it is tender, then add the spinach and let it sweat in the butter until it has wilted down. Bring the stock to the boil and pour on to the spinach. Allow to simmer until the spinach is completely tender but still green. Sieve through the finest blade of a mouli-légumes or put in the liquidizer. Then beat the egg yolks in a separate bowl with some lemon juice and gradually add 1 cup of hot stock, beating all the time. Return this liquid to the soup and heat very gently, stirring all the time until very slightly thickened. Do not let it boil after the eggs have been added. Season and serve, with a strip of lemon peel in each bowl. This soup is delicious when it is chilled and served with a whirl of sour cream.

Eggs Florentine (*for 6*)

3lb ($1\frac{1}{2}$kg) spinach	salt, pepper
a sprinkling of flour	1 pint ($\frac{3}{4}$l; 2 cups) Mornay
$\frac{1}{4}$ pint ($\frac{1}{8}$l; $\frac{1}{2}$ cup) thick cream	sauce
	6 eggs

Cook the spinach until it is just tender, then drain it well. Return it to the pan.

Mix the flour into the cream and mix both into the spinach. Simmer over low heat, stirring from time to time, until the flour has thickened and absorbed the water which still runs from the spinach. Season and keep hot.

Meanwhile, make the Mornay sauce and keep this hot too. Next poach the eggs, and keep them warm in a bowl of hot water (not too hot as they must not go on cooking).

Put the spinach in an oval gratin dish, lay the well-drained eggs on top and pour the cheese sauce over them. Brown quickly under the heat.

Spinach pancakes

Roll cooked, well-drained spinach into thin pancakes, and place the rolls side by side in a buttered fireproof dish. Cover with a Mornay sauce, add a layer of grated cheese, and brown in a medium oven.

Alternatively, and more spectacularly, spread less thin pancakes, one by one, with a thick layer of spinach, building up a sort of layer cake. Use Mornay sauce as you would icing. Put in the oven until flecked with brown, and serve in wedges.

Potage de santé (*for 6*)

'Health soup' and delicious in a particularly green, fresh summery way.

Cook 1 chopped onion gently in oil until golden, and add 1 handful each of chopped sorrel and spinach, 1 head of lettuce, 4 pints ($2\frac{1}{2}$l; 8 cups) of hot stock, and 4 potatoes. Simmer for

---

How to grow spinach

Summer spinach is light green, winter spinach is slightly darker. Both are delicious and high in calcium, iron and vitamin C content. For a constant supply of this invaluable vegetable, seed is sown in good rich ground from spring to early summer. Drills 1in (2·5cm) deep should be 12in (30cm) apart. Thin as soon as the plants are large enough to handle. Each sowing of summer spinach takes about five weeks to grow and gives about three weeks' picking, so seed may be sown every three weeks if you like. Spinach needs a lot of moisture and mulching. There are varieties of perpetual spinach which are easy to grow; they produce leaves all the year round and are sown in late spring and summer. True to their name the plants come up year after year. (Swiss chard is another variation with enormous spinach-like leaves and broad silver mid ribs which are useful when the leaves are tough and leathery and no longer very appetizing. Simply cut them near the stem, strip off the old greenery and proceed as for leeks.)

1. Spinach likes well-manured soil

2. From spring to early summer sow in 1in (2·5cm) drills

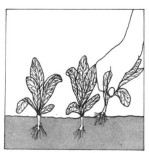

3. Thin, hoe and water well, using the thinnings for salad

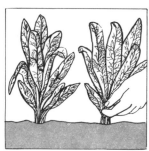

4. Pick over regularly, always from the bottom

about 45 minutes. Sieve, blend (only for the merest second) or put through the mouli, add chervil and a dash of cream.

Spinach purée

Cook the washed spinach until tender, and drain. Put some milk and butter in the blender, add the spinach, salt, pepper and a pinch of grated nutmeg, and blend until puréed. Before serving, lightly stir in a little cream.

Stuffed spinach leaves

1–1½lb (450–675g) large spinach leaves with no holes	1 onion, chopped
	1 shallot, finely chopped
	1 clove of garlic, crushed
½lb (225g; 1 cup) good minced beef	salt, pepper
	cayenne pepper
2½oz (65g; 1¼ cups) rice, boiled	juice of 1 lemon
	1½oz (35g; ¼ cup) butter or oil

Wash the spinach. Combine the meat, cooked rice, onion and shallot, and garlic. Mix well, seasoning with a dash of cayenne, salt and pepper. Make small balls. Remove the spinach leaves from their stalks, wash well and dip in boiling salted water for a few seconds. Use one or two leaves to neatly envelop and parcel the balls. Melt the butter in a heavy pan. Place the spinach parcels in the pan, close together, so that they do not unroll. Sprinkle with lemon juice. Cover, and simmer *very gently* for 2 hours.

Spinach salad (*for 4–6*)

2lb (900g) very young spinach	4 bacon rashers
oil, vinegar	garlic, if you like
	salt, pepper

Pick all the smallest inner leaves from the spinach (keep the large ones for something else). Wash them and dry very thoroughly on a cloth without bruising. Put them in a large salad bowl. Make a good French dressing. Cut the bacon into dice and fry in its own fat until crisp. Pour the bacon together with its fat over the spinach, add 3 or 4 tablespoons of French dressing, toss the salad and serve immediately. Otherwise keep the bacon hot and add it at the last moment before serving.

Green gnocchi (*plenty for 4*)

1lb (450g) fresh spinach, cooked, chopped, and squeezed dry	8oz (225g; 1 cup) cottage or cream cheese
3 potatoes, boiled and mashed	3 tablespoons grated Parmesan cheese
2 egg yolks	¼ teaspoon salt
4oz (110g; ½ cup) butter	3 tablespoons flour
	seasoning

Mix together the spinach, potatoes, egg yolks, sieved cottage cheese, half the butter, most of the Parmesan cheese, salt and

flour. Roll on a floured board into a long finger-thin sausage and cut this into pieces 2in (5cm) long. Cook a few pieces at a time in boiling salted water. When pieces rise to the surface, remove with a wire spoon. Keep the water boiling and repeat the process until all the gnocchi are cooked. Place in a fireproof dish, melt the rest of the butter and pour over the gnocchi, and sprinkle the rest of the Parmesan cheese over the top. Brown in the oven, and serve very hot.

These gnocchi are softer and lighter than the ones made with semolina. They make a wonderful lunch, covered with home-made tomato sauce. Both may need heating in a hot oven before serving.

Stir-fried spinach

Nothing brings out the juicy green of spinach so well as the Chinese way of quick-frying it. For this glistening dish, heat vegetable oil – enough to cover the bottom of a deep pan large enough to hold all the spinach. Crush a clove of garlic, and put it and the spinach into the pan, stirring hard over a high heat, for 3 minutes. Lower the heat, add a knob of butter, a pinch of salt and one of sugar, and keep on turning the spinach until the butter has melted. Serve at once.

Eggs with marbled spinach sauce (*ingredients for 1 person*)

4 tablespoons Mornay sauce	1 egg per person
	½ hollowed soft roll
1 tablespoon cream	clarified butter
2 tablespoons well-drained, chopped cooked spinach	2 teaspoons grated cheese, Parmesan if possible

Make the Mornay sauce and keep it warm; pour about 1 tablespoon of cream into the pan – it will prevent a skin from forming. Prepare the spinach and keep it warm. Boil the eggs for exactly 5 minutes, placing the saucepan under the cold tap as soon as the time is up. Fry the hollowed round rolls, in clarified butter, tilting them a little so that the sides come in contact with the butter. Draw off the heat, quickly shell the eggs and place one in each of the hollowed rolls. Dish out on heated plates. Stir the spinach (together with cream still resting on the surface) lightly into the sauce, and pour the stiff marbled mixture over the eggs and sprinkle with grated cheese.

SORREL *Rumex acetosa*

This plant, also called sour grass in the USA, is common in damp meadows. It is extensively grown in its cultivated form in France for use in mixed salads and soups. It is sown in spring, in rows 10in (25cm) apart and thinned to 12in (30cm) between the plants. It likes light soil and a sunny position, and will grow knee-high, with arrow-shaped leaves. The flowers should be cut off to prevent the plant from running to seed and becoming tough.

Sorrel is a valuable source of iron and vitamin C, but

Sorrel
Rumex acetosa

as it contains oxalic acid, it should be eaten in moderation. Its taste is tart and tangy, rather like spinach with lemon; its bitterness, however, is blunted if it is used together with lettuce. (In the making of 'sallets' says John Evelyn, 'it imparts a grateful quickness to the rest, as supplying the want of oranges and lemons.')

Sorrel soup (*for 4–6; very useful for lifting jaded appetites*)

1lb (450g) sorrel	1½ pints (1l; 3 cups)
1 small round lettuce	chicken stock
1 onion	2–3 egg yolks
1 heaped tablespoon butter	2–3 tablespoons tiny,
salt, pepper	freshly made croûtons

Wash the sorrel and lettuce and chop them coarsely. Chop the onion and soften it in the butter in a large saucepan for 5–10 minutes. Put the sorrel and lettuce in with the onion and allow to wilt – the sorrel melts and changes colour from bright green to pond green immediately, the lettuce takes a little longer. Pour on the boiling stock, season and simmer, uncovered, until the sorrel and lettuce are cooked through, about 10–15 minutes. Sieve the soup through the mouli-légumes or sieve. A liquidizer is not effective with this soup as it cannot cope with the hair-like fibres in the sorrel. Return the soup to the pan and heat it without boiling. Beat the egg yolks in a bowl, stir in a few tablespoons of the soup and return to the pan. Stir continually over a very low heat, without boiling, until slightly thickened.

Sorrel, when it is cooked, already has a beautiful velvety

consistency; the egg yolks make it a little richer. Serve with a knob of butter or a spoonful of cream in each plate and a sprinkling of very hot croûtons.

Sorrel omelette (*for 4*)

1 large handful young sorrel	1 knob butter
	salt, pepper
6 eggs, lightly beaten	½ tablespoon olive oil
2 tablespoons milk	4 tablespoons thick cream

Strip the sorrel leaves from the central rib, and cut into fine strips. Mix together with the eggs, milk and seasoning. Heat the butter and the oil together in an omelette pan (the oil will prevent the butter from burning as it gets to the sizzling stage), and when you see vapour rising from the pan, quickly cook the omelette. When it is cooked below but still moist on top, tip it out – folding it over – on to a heated serving dish. Quickly make a deep incision with a sharp pointed knife on the uppermost surface, pour in the thick cream and serve.

DANDELION *Leontodon taraxacum*

Wild or cultivated dandelion leaves, raw or cooked, were no strangers to the kitchens of the past. Blanched and puréed, blended with cream and butter, young dandelion leaves can be eaten with hard-boiled eggs or cold ham.

The uncooked greenery of the dandelion, so well-known a diuretic that it is rudely called *pissenlit* in France, where it is sold in large quantities on market stalls, was nonetheless recommended in Culpeper's *Herbal* as a leaf 'that helpeth to procure rest and sleep.' However, we learn from a nineteenth-century work on plant lore that 'to dream of dandelions betokens misfortune.' Whichever school of thought you follow, there is nothing so good as a salad made of the young leaves.

Pissenlit au lard

Pick over the young plants. As they grow best on really poor soil, vestiges of sand often cling to them, indiscernible to the naked eye, but gritty on the tooth. The thing which makes this salad special is that the entire small, juicy plants go into a Vinaigrette over which is thrown a panful of sizzling little pieces of salt pork or bacon with their fat.

NASTURTIUM *Tropaeolum majus* and *minus*

Always a pleasure to see in the garden, nasturtiums are useful as a salad plant. The young leaves are very peppery (and only the young ones should be used). Like watercress, they are good in salads, especially with cucumber, when used in moderation. Pickled nasturtium seedpods are sometimes substituted for capers.

LAND CRESS *Barbarea praecox*

Land cress, also called winter cress, tastes like watercress; it is sown in late summer and needs protection in severe winters. Like all cresses it grows quickly and can be eaten 8–10 weeks from sowing.

Cress soup (*for 6*)

Put 2–3 large potatoes and 1 onion, peeled and roughly chopped, into a large pan. Add 1½ pints (1l; 3 cups) cold stock, bring to the boil and simmer for 15–20 minutes; now throw in 2 bunches of washed cress, stalks and all, and cook until tender but still a good green. Sieve all this, helping it through the mouli-légumes by moistening with some milk. Now add enough milk to make the soup a good consistency – about ¾ pint (½l; 1½ cups). Return the soup to the heat, season and heat through. Serve with a knob of butter and a sprig of cress in each plate.

Eggs with cress (*for 4*)

8 eggs	½ pint (¼l; 1 cup) light stock
2 thick slices stale bread	1 tablespoon flour
knob of butter	knob of butter
1 clove of garlic, crushed	cream to taste
for the sauce :	salt
1 big bunch cress	pepper

Poach the eggs, put them in a shallow dish and keep them in a warm place. Chop the crusts from the bread and cut each slice into quarters. Fry the bread in hot butter until golden.

Rub the garlic into the croûtons and keep them hot too.

To make the sauce, chop the cress and simmer it in the stock for 5 minutes, then push the mixture through the fine blade of a mouli. Make a roux with the flour and butter, add cress purée and stir until the flour is cooked and the sauce is smooth. Add the cream and season with salt and pepper. Pour the sauce over the eggs and arrange the croûtons round them. This makes a good first course, or a light lunch.

MUSTARD AND CRESS
Brassica alba and *Lepidium sativum*

Mustard and cress cannot be left out. It is grown – as a child's first gardening venture – outside or inside, upstairs, downstairs, on a wet flannel or paper tissue, in saucers or trays on the window sill; and it goes into sandwiches and salads.

STINGING NETTLE *Urtica dioica* or *piluifera*

This public enemy number one produces young leaves which are docile, tonic in effect, and rich in vitamin A and minerals. Its sting (for which it was prized in old herbals, where people afflicted with gout or sciatica were advised to whip their afflicted parts with this plant) disappears the minute boiling water touches the leaves and stems. Nettle tisane – made like tea, but using fresh nettles – was credited with immense health-giving properties, from restoring hair to promoting vigour in old age. Svelte Italians, even today, prepare their bodies for the beach and the tourist season by going on a diet of stewed nettle shoots in March. By May, the unflattering fat produced by a rich winter diet has disappeared. Nettle poultices are recommended for easing toothache and, sprinkled with salt, are good 'against the biting of dogs', but it is not clear whether they are curative or preventative. Nettle soup, made like sorrel or spinach soup, is very good, with a flavour all its own, but only young shoots should be used – and pickers should use scissors and wear gloves.

LETTUCE *Lactuca sativa*

Lettuce, for most people the synonym for salad, has of course been eaten for centuries, and its popularity has remained constant.

It was well known in Egypt, Greece and Rome. Aristoxemus, famous for his home-grown lettuces, used to water them with wine, and said that it improved their flavour. It was a lettuce salad into which Cleopatra tossed her pearl. Her intention was not to dissolve her jewel in vinegar – the myth is based on this famous occurrence – but to prove that her banquet was every bit as expensive as one given earlier by Pompey.

The Romans ate lettuce as a panacea of all ills. The Emperor Augustus's physician, prescribing a lettuce diet, was thought to have saved his patient's life by doing so. The word 'lettuce' is a corruption of the Latin *lactuca* – milk – which it bears because of the white juice it exudes when cut. This milk, it was thought, helped to keep away drunkenness, and lettuce was invariably served at the end of a meal before the serious drinking began. The fashion changed in due course, and lettuce appeared more logically at the beginning of Roman meals, and became the first recorded hors d'oeuvre. (The modern superstition that a glass of milk taken before a party helps to keep one sober may have its origins in the lettuces of Ancient Rome.)

ENDIVE *Cichorium endivia*

Endive (called chicory in the USA) is another good salad plant, a great rosette of jagged leaves. Seeds are sown in early to mid summer, in a seed bed or in the open ground, and thinned to 12in (30cm). Three or four months after sowing, the plants will be fully grown, and if they are not to turn bitter, they must be blanched by keeping the light off them. This may be done simply with inverted flowerpots, or with a plate laid across the middle of the plant. Aim for a succession of plants that can be eaten when the central leaves are a pale yellowy white.

The best dressing is a smooth one that coats the leaves well, either a traditional Vinaigrette using a lot of oil and little vinegar, or a mixture of a little oil, lemon juice and thin cream (top of the milk will do).

In France, where they call the endive *chicorée*, it has long been a popular plant. Colbert, Louis XIV's great minister, dismayed the owner of a splendid new garden at the height of the garden mania in Versailles. No expense was spared to lay out a magical park. On his tour of the garden, however, Colbert barely glanced at the rare plants or the *parterre* of grass; he ignored the play of the fountain and the sculpted figures around it, and the artificial waterfall with coral and mother-of-pearl shelves; he signified no interest in the avenues *à perte de vue*. Only when he reached the sunken kitchen garden did his heart quicken; he exclaimed with pleasure, at last, '*Voilà, voilà une belle chicorée*.'

CORN SALAD OR LAMB'S LETTUCE
Valerianella locusta

A valuable winter salad, very small, with leaves 2in (5cm) long. It is particularly good dressed like dandelion, or in a traditional Vinaigrette and mixed with boiled beetroot. Seeds are sown in late summer in succession, thinning to 9in (23cm) apart.

ROCKET *Eruca sativa*

Another popular salad plant in Europe. It has pungent-tasting leaves and will grow almost anywhere. Seeds are sown from early to late summer; it grows 12–24in (30–60cm) high and has delicious-smelling cream or lilac flowers. The leaves are used alone or mixed with lettuce and other green leaves. Go easy on the seasoning: rocket is quite peppery on its own and does not need additional spicing up. Even mustard must be used with caution.

How to grow lettuce

Ideally, lettuce is sown frequently and a little at a time so that you can eat it all through the summer and autumn. The seeds germinate very quickly and easily. They may be sown in boxes and seed beds and transplanted, or go into rows in the open ground (*in situ*) and thinned. Thinnings are used in salads and soups (with sorrel, for instance). Begin to sow outside in spring and continue when you have a spare moment, every three weeks or so, until late summer. Some varieties are very strong and hardy, and sown in early autumn will go through the winter to eat in spring. Lettuce is always best grown quickly, so it needs good soil and a lot of water. There are three main varieties; crips hearts with curled leaves, very unlikely to run to seed; butter heads which are soft and round and melting in the mouth; and Cos, the crisp, tall-leaved variety. These need to be picked at their peak because, once over it, they shoot up with amazing rapidity. Of course they can be eaten even then, but they will taste bitter. There are some specially bred for any time and position; be sure to get the right variety and do not sow a greenhouse or frame variety outside. Seed is sown ½in (1·2cm) deep and the plants thinned to about 10in (25cm) according to size.

1. Start lettuce off in boxes; sow thinly

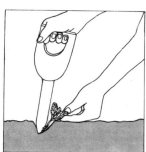

2. Transplant when seedlings are large enough to handle

3. Water well; lettuce must grow fast to be tender

4. Do not leave too long in the ground, or lettuce shoot up and become bitter

FUNGI

Cèpe
Boletus

Champignon
Psalliota campestris

Nothing is nicer than the taste of freshly gathered mushrooms with their damp woodland smell. But it is important never to go out picking unless you know for sure *exactly* what you are looking for, as the most dangerous of all fungi are those which are most like edible ones. And with fungi, dangerous can not only mean highly toxic but possibly fatal. So never take risks. Always pick with someone who knows, or go armed with a good mushroom book. When you do you will

learn what marvellous treats are in store for you. All over Europe many fungi are eaten after gathering as a matter of course; in Britain it is only the field mushroom which is widely known and gathered from pastures and fields.

There are many more which should be made use of with the proper care. Chanterelles (*Cantharellus cibarius*), with their egg-yellow, funnel-shaped caps, are delicious. They smell like apricots, are less tender than mushrooms and need longer cooking. The giant Puffball (*Lycoperdon giganteum*) looks like a smooth white balloon and is good when young. The Cèpe (*Boletus edulis*) – our 'penny bun' – is large, and eaten a lot in Europe in soups and stews and sautéed *à la bordelaise* with parsley and garlic. It is found in woods, particularly pine woods, in summer and autumn. There is also the shaggy Parasol (*Lepiota procera*), with a scaly cap and long, stout white stem; the Blewit (*Tricholoma saevum*) and the Fairy Ring Champignon (*Marasmius oreades*) which forms the magic rings on lawns and grass. The stems of these should not be eaten because they are tough, whereas the caps taste good and dry well for flavouring. But never take a chance with anything you are the slightest bit doubtful about. Going by smell, or by eye – to see if the cut surface changes colour, or to wait for a silver spoon to turn black in the case of a suspicious specimen – is no substitute for sound knowledge which it is not hard to acquire.

Of all the fungi, the black truffle is the most prized. It grows underground. The best ones come from the Périgord district of France. They are rare and capricious in so far as they may desert their old haunts to grow in unsuspected places, and they are not so much picked as hunted, with the help of truffle-hounds and specially trained pigs. The pigs are efficient rooters, but also great truffle eaters, and do not always feel sufficiently rewarded by a snoutful of acorns, much to the dismay of their masters who occasionally see the 'black diamonds' disappear down the animals' throats.

Then there are white truffles from Northern Italy, fairly hard to find and less powerful of aroma; but they, too, are capable of pervading any dish with the unique truffle taste. Eggs, after just spending some time in their vicinity, will produce an omelette tasting strongly of truffles, although the truffle itself may not even have been cut, let alone added.

The dish of kings, *Truffes au champagne*, does however need large handsome black truffles, unpeeled but well cleaned. These go into the pot with 2 tablespoons of mixed, chopped vegetables, cooked in butter, to each pound, and are cooked in champagne for 15 minutes. Then they go into little silver dishes, while the pan juices are thickened with thick brown veal gravy. This is poured over the truffles and the *cassolets* are kept hot (without coming to the boil) for a few minutes before serving.

All fungi are rich in potassium and phosphorus, and very low in calories.

Basic treatment

Fungi should always be used freshly gathered; they deteriorate too fast to be left lying about. Whether to peel them or not is a matter of choice – if they are very fresh, this is hardly necessary, though the ends of the stems and any ragged edges of the caps should be trimmed off with a sharp knife. The gills underneath fully opened umbrellas are always best pared away. Mushrooms and fungi can be diced, sliced, or left whole, according to their size and your recipe.

To bring out their individual flavours – and it is surprising how different the various species taste – it is best to sauté them gently in melted, not sizzling, butter to which a drop or two of lemon juice, a dash of water and some salt, have been added. This is the ideal way for small quantities, which, provided that the heat is low enough, will literally cook in their own juices. If a large amount of fungi is cooked, water is usually allowed to predominate in the liquor. The classic *blanc à champignon* is made up of $\frac{1}{2}$ pint ($\frac{1}{4}$l; 1 cup) water, 2 tablespoons butter, the juice of half a small lemon and a pinch of salt. This is enough for 1lb (450g) of mushrooms or fungi. They should be plunged into the liquid when it boils, and allowed to boil fairly rapidly for 5 minutes, by which time they will be tender, and will have absorbed much of the liquid. The rest should not be poured away, but thickened with a roux for soups or sauces.

Chanterelles cooked in this way, and liberally sprinkled with parsley, go wonderfully well with lightly scrambled eggs – serve this on buttered toast topped with a mound of this golden vegetable, for late-summer lunch. Cèpes, in the countries where they grow profusely, are served as a vegetable course in their own right. In the wooded parts of Germany, a thick mushroom soup made of cèpes is often on the menu – each spoonful solid with the little aromatic dice.

Risotto con funghi (*for 6*)

A good Italian lunch dish on its own or with a green salad.

2 onions	1 glass white wine
2 heaped tablespoons butter	salt, pepper
1lb (450g) mushrooms	2 heaped tablespoons
1lb (450g) Italian rice	grated Parmesan cheese
2 pints ($1\frac{1}{4}$l; 4 cups)	a little cream
chicken stock	parsley

Chop the onions finely. Melt the butter and soften the onions while you cut the mushrooms into quarters. You can slice them finely but they tend to disappear and lose their texture. Throw them in with the onions and stir them round until they are coated with butter. Add the wine and let it bubble fast until it has evaporated. Now add the rice, stir it round for a minute and pour on half the stock. As this is absorbed add a little more from time to time, and season to taste. When the rice is cooked, after 25–30 minutes stir in half the cheese and some more butter. The risotto is a warm beige with pale mushrooms here and there. You can add a little cream at this point, for the risotto should be creamy and moist, not dry like most other rice dishes.

Serve with grated Parmesan cheese, a knob of butter and a grating of black pepper to each plate and a generous sprinkling of parsley.

Champignons à la crème

Simmer the mushrooms until soft, then add enough fresh cream to make them float. Boil briskly until the cream has almost disappeared. Add a little chopped onion previously softened in butter, stir well, and finish with a final dash of fresh cream. A sprinkling of fresh – it must be fresh, or it will

have no taste – paprika looks nice and transforms the dish into *Champignons à la hongroise.*

Champignons à la Provençal

Use little white button mushrooms, or dice the larger variety. Simmer in a little light stock, raising the heat at the very end so that the juices in the pan are re-absorbed. Lower the heat, and add 1 crushed clove of garlic and 1 teaspoon of finely chopped shallots – stir until these latest additions have turned transparent, add parsley, and serve.

Fillet of pork in pastry with duxelles

Duxelles – finely chopped mushrooms – are used in any number of *haute cuisine* dishes, and invariably appear in meat cooked *en croûte.* This addition stretches it marvellously, enabling a modest pork fillet weighing barely 1lb (450g) to feed a dinner party of six, particularly if puff pastry is used, which is not traditional but very good.

½lb (225g) puff pastry	bunch of parsley
pork fillet, about 9–10 in (23–25cm) long	1 large or 2 small onions
	2–3 slices of bread
10 medium mushrooms	seasoning
1 egg	knob of butter

Roll out the pastry into a hole-less rectangle 4in (10cm) longer than the meat, and place it in a greased roasting tin. Heat some butter in a large shallow pan, and seal the meat on all sides. Place it in the centre of the sheet of pastry. Now chop the mushrooms, parsley and onion as minutely as possible, and place in a basin. Crumble the bread, moistened and de-crusted, into the mixture, then combine the ingredients and season. Beat the egg in a cup and stir most of it in, saving just a little for glazing the pastry. Spoon the *duxelles* on top of the fillet, and parcel the whole by sealing together the long edges. Leave room for the *duxelles* to swell – you do not want to make a tight package, but a loose one with firm 'seams'. Neatly tuck in the short edges and press well down, because the *duxelles* will try to escape through any loophole they can find. Brush over the pastry with the remaining egg, and bake in a moderate oven (Reg 4/350°F) until puffy and golden.

Creamed mushrooms *(for 3–4)*

½lb (225g) mushrooms	2 tablespoons flour
2 slices lemon	salt, pepper
1 teaspoon mixed herbs	4 tablespoons cream
2 tablespoons butter	buttered wholemeal toast

Wipe the mushrooms and put them in a pan with the lemon, herbs and a little water. Cook them until they are tender, then remove the herbs and lemon, and strain and put the liquid on one side. Heat the butter, cook the flour in it with a little salt and pepper, then add the mushroom stock and cream to make a thick sauce. Stir in the mushrooms and serve on buttered wholemeal toast sprinkled with parsley and a dash more of lemon juice.

How to grow mushrooms

Mushrooms do not grow from seed but from spores and can be cultivated indoors and out from spawn. This is available in various proprietory brands. These are always packaged along with detailed instructions which beginners should follow to the letter. Old hands will have worked out their own private technique, and they will also know which part of the house, shed or greenhouse is most conducive to mushroom-growing. The spawn can sometimes be bought together with mushroom-growing compost – this again is most useful for people who do not want to start the laborious business of making up their own with horse manure and wheat straw sandwiched in alternate layers. Novices should always start in a small way.

Those who own lawns might try planting culture spawn under the turf and pray that nature will provide the right conditions. Nature can be assisted in so far as the spawn, even under the grass, does best if you remove a 10in (25cm) square of turf and the topsoil below, filling up the resulting cavity with strawy manure or compost. Into this insert a walnut-sized chunk of spawn, replace the turf and trust to luck. Indoors and out, mushrooms should be harvested by twisting them out from the soil before they are fully opened. They should never be cut, because their decaying stumps can spoil the soil. If they are grown indoors in box or bucket, the holes created by picking should be filled up so that the next lot remains warm and the moisture on which they depend does not evaporate.

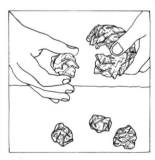

1. Divide mushroom spawn into walnut-sized pieces

2. Tuck into mushroom-growing compost (or under turf)

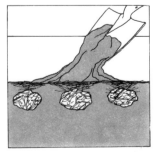

3. Cover the pieces of spawn well

4. Harvest by twisting the stems

Mushroom and potato stew (*for 4*)

Cook 8 peeled, quartered potatoes until barely tender. Drain, saving the liquid, and set aside. Melt until it sizzles a large knob of butter, and toss 2 handfuls of mushrooms, small or cut, about in the pan until they are coated with brown butter. Lower the heat, add 2 tablespoons of flour, stirring it until you have a roux in which the mushrooms are the only lumps. Gradually stir in enough potato water to achieve a creamy consistency. Add the cooked potatoes, simmer for a few minutes, season and finish off with a dash of cream.

Sauce bourguignonne

Burgundy, the gastronomic centre of France, is a paradise for mushrooms. Dishes *à la bourguignonne* invariably contain them, and a good deal of red wine, usually served with a braised joint, the sauce should be added to the meat 15 minutes before it has finished cooking.

For a good ½ pint (¼l; 1 cup) of sauce, reduce 1 pint (½l; 2 cups) of red wine by half, boiling it rapidly, having added a spoonful of chopped shallots and a good handful of chopped mushrooms (this is a good dish for using mushroom stalks, or even skins if you are a mushroom peeler). Having prepared this *fumet*, thicken it to the desired consistency with *beurre manié* – small kneaded pellets of butter and flour which are added one by one – and add it to the casserole in which the meat is cooking. Using a fork, blend the pan juices with the wine sauce, and allow the aroma to permeate the meat.

Pommes grand'mère

In this dish, a very few chopped mushrooms transform ordinary sauté potatoes into a very special dish. It is particularly good with roast chicken. Begin by sautéeing a chopped onion in butter in which a slice or two of chopped up fatty bacon has been rendered. Add the raw chopped mushrooms and the boiled sliced potatoes when the onion is just beginning to colour, and cook over a gentle heat for about 5 minutes, turning and stirring so that all the ingredients come in contact with the bottom of the pan.

Mushrooms à la grecque

These are simmered for a short time – about 10 minutes – in a liquid prepared beforehand:

Simmer ¼ pint (⅛l; ½ cup) olive oil, ¼ pint (⅛l; ½ cup) water, juice of 1 lemon, 1 bay leaf, 1 teaspoon thyme, 1 teaspoon coriander seeds, 4 skinned, chopped, seeded tomatoes, and 1 sliced clove of garlic, in a wide shallow pan for 10 minutes. Add the mushrooms, which may be small buttons, left whole; medium buttons, halved; large ones, quartered. When they have simmered, let them cool in the liquor; a lovely hors d'oeuvre.

Raw mushroom salad (*for 4–6*)

1lb (450g) tiny white button mushrooms	salt
½ pint (¼l; 1 cup) sour cream	pepper
	1 lemon

Trim the mushrooms, and if they are the slightest bit brown they will need peeling. As you peel each one, rub it with the cut lemon. When they are all clean and white, slice each one thinly and put into a china bowl. Keep the stalks on so that each slice shows you a tiny mushroom in section. When they are all sliced mix in the sour cream and season lightly. This should be a delicate salad. If you like to add a little more lemon juice with the cream to sharpen it up, that can be good too.

Stuffed mushrooms

Reckon 2 reasonably large – but not fully opened – mushrooms per person, or 4 smaller ones. If you offer this dish as an hors d'oeuvre, use small plates, otherwise it may look a bit pathetic, which would be a pity because it is extremely delicious. It also makes a good accompaniment to veal or poultry. For 4 people, remove the stalks from 8 mushrooms, chop finely and set aside. Sauté the caps very gently indeed for a few minutes. Put them stalk-side up in a buttered, shallow baking dish. For the stuffing, sauté the chopped

stalks, 2 shallots, 2 onions, and 1 clove of garlic for 5 minutes, and stir this mixture into a bowl containing 1 large egg beaten in 1 tablespoon of cream. Mix well, season, and add 2 tablespoons of chopped parsley. Spoon this mixture on top of the mushrooms, and let it set in a medium oven. It will take about 10 minutes. Serve at once.

Mushrooms with coriander seeds

Reckon 4 mushrooms, 4 coriander seeds per person. Squeeze a little lemon juice over some unpeeled white mushrooms which you have left whole, halved or quartered according to their size. Warm some oil in a sauté pan, and add the crushed coriander seeds, one bay leaf and seasoning. Let the mixture cool, and serve as a starter or a salad.

Mushrooms with garlic butter (*for 4*)

Choose very large caps, but ones that are not quite flattened and opened. Trim off the stalks and scrape off the gills. Place them, cavity upwards, on a shallow fireproof dish in which they fit snugly. Mash 4 tablespoons butter with 2 heaped tablespoons each of chopped parsley and chives, together with 3 crushed cloves of garlic, salt and pepper. Then place the dish in a medium oven for about 10 minutes, just enough time for you to cut thickish slices of French bread, and to fry these in a mixture of oil and butter until golden on both sides.

Mushroom soufflé (*for 4*)

1lb (450g) mushrooms	salt and white pepper
2 tablespoons butter	extra butter
2 tablespoons flour	lemon juice
4 tablespoons cream	2 eggs, separated

Sauté the mushrooms in a little butter for a few minutes until they are swimming in their own juice. Strain and keep the juice. Make a Béchamel sauce with the butter, flour, cream and mushroom juice. Add this to the sautéed mushrooms. Season with salt, pepper and a squeeze of lemon juice. Beat the egg yolks and stir into the mixture, and then fold in the stiffly beaten egg whites. Turn into a deep buttered dish, preheat the oven to Reg 5/375°F, put in the oven and cook for 30 minutes.

Mushroom omelette

Gently sauté a few mushrooms with a finely chopped onion. Lightly beat 2 eggs and season them with salt and black pepper. Melt a knob of butter in the omelette pan and then turn up the heat. Mix the eggs into the melted butter with a fork and shake the eggs in the pan to make sure they are evenly cooked. Spread with most of the mushrooms. Fold the omelette in half and turn it swiftly on to a warm plate. Scatter the remaining mushrooms on top; sprinkle with parsley and chives, previously chopped.

Try to reserve a special pan solely for omelette-making purposes. That way omelettes will never stick.

FRUIT

Tomato
Lycopersicon esculentum

Sweet peppers and aubergines, which are also called egg-plants because of a pure white variety shaped like the egg of an enormous goose, still have something of the exotic about them, but it seems strange that our old friends the tomatoes were once regarded with very suspicious eyes. And not so very long ago either, Marie Rundell, the first English best-selling cookery book writer, whose book *A New System of Domestic Cookery* was published in 1808, gave a single recipe involving tomatoes, and that for Catsup; Eliza Acton, publishing in 1845, gave several, but all for cooked tomatoes; no one would have dreamt of eating them raw.

TOMATO *Lycopersicon esculentum*

The tomato came to Europe from South America with the Spanish and Portuguese sixteenth-century discoverers. They introduced it to their fellow-countrymen, who ate it boiled in oil, pepper and salt. The Italians gave it a warm welcome and married it to the noodles which Marco Polo had previously brought from China. They called it the *pomo di morto* – the apple of the Moor – because of its Spanish provenance.

This name became the basis for the later glamorous names acquired by the tomato (itself derived from the Mexican *tomatl*): it became *pomme d'amour* to the French, who instantly invested it with the usual aphrodisiac properties. In the Perigord district, tomato soup, laced with vermicelli, became a ritual *soupe des noces*, to be carried in procession to the bridal chamber. In Italy, *pomo di moro* soon became *pomodoro*, from which it was a short step to the golden apple, as it was sometimes called in England, instead of love-apple.

Gerard was the first Englishman to report on the tomato. 'The fruit is of a red shining colour,' he said, 'the bignesse of a good egg or pippin.' Since he was growing tomatoes in his London garden from a present of seeds sent from its native land, it must have been a hot summer. In general, the tomato did not take too kindly to the uncertain English climate, and its wider cultivation had to wait for Paxton (of subsequent Crystal Palace fame) to build for the Duke of Devonshire at Chatsworth the great prefabricated glass houses which were the forerunners of greenhouses every-where. Tomatoes, very rich in vitamin C are in the lowest group for calories, fewer than 25 a helping.

Basic treatment

Wipe clean, and remove the stalks. For baking, put them in a shallow fireproof dish, stalk end down. Brush with oil, season well, and cut through the skin, making a little cross on the top to prevent the tomato from exploding. Baking time in a medium oven can be anything from 15 to 35 minutes, depending on the size and age of the tomato and the density of stuffing, if any. To grill or broil, cut the tomato in half, dot with butter, season, and expose to the heat for about 5 minutes.

Salad: It is altogether better to serve tomatoes separately. They contain a great deal of liquid, and will make the most stout-hearted lettuce wilt.

Many recipes call for peeled tomatoes, and there are two easy ways to peel them. Either pop them into boiling water for a few seconds, or swivel them, on the end of an old fork, over high heat until the skin starts to blister. The skin and the tomato will then part company without a struggle.

How to grow tomatoes

There are different tomato varieties for indoors and out. There are even miniature tomatoes for window boxes, as attractive as they are sweet to eat. When you plant tomatoes outside, pray for a really good summer. A lot of sun is needed and outdoor tomatoes like a warm border – if possible sheltered by a wall. They also need plenty of water and mulching. You can buy your tomato plants, but to raise them from seed sow 3 seeds in a tiny pot and thin to one; or sow in boxes under glass and prick off into pots. Pot-grown seedlings are usually sturdier when planting-out time comes, which is early summer. Stakes go in with the plants, but bush tomatoes need little or no support. Remove side shoots regularly and cut off the growing point of the plant to encourage the fruit to ripen. Straw under the plants acts as a mulch and protects any fallen fruit.

1. After gradual hardening off, plant by a stake

2. Remove side shoots and keep moist

Italian tomato soup

The thick, glutinous tinned red liquid that passes as tomato soup is very far removed from the real thing, which is surprisingly easy to make.

Reduce to a purée 1½lb (675g) of chopped, skinned tomatoes in a little olive oil over low heat. Add a crushed clove of garlic and some fresh basil or parsley. Cook for about 5 minutes,

then add 1 pint (¾l; 2 cups) of light stock, salt, pepper and a pinch of sugar to bring out the flavour of the tomatoes. Cook for a further 5 minutes, then serve with a sprinkling of chopped parsley. (A fresh and flavoursome soup, this can be served iced in the summer.)

Cream of tomato soup (*for 4*)

1½lb (675g) ripe tomatoes	1 bay leaf
2oz (50g; ¼ cup) butter	1 clove of garlic
small bunch spring onions	salt, pepper
1 pint (¾l; 2 cups) light stock	pinch of sugar
	2 tablespoons cream

Peel, chop and de-seed the tomatoes. Melt the butter in a heavy saucepan, and fry the finely chopped spring onions and garlic until soft and transparent. Add the stock, the bay leaf, and the tomatoes. Bring to the boil, lower the heat, and simmer with the lid on for about 15 minutes until the tomatoes have collapsed. At this point, remove the bay leaf. You can either push the soup through a sieve or a mouli, or leave it as it is. Season with salt, pepper and sugar. In a separate pan, heat most of the cream and stir it into the soup. Serve with a final swirl of cream.

Orange and tomato soup

These fruits complement each other well. Proceed as for cream of tomato soup, but before adding the cream, squeeze into the pan the juice of an orange. Serve with a garnish of shredded and blanched orange rind.

Gazpacho (*for 3–4*)

A traditional Spanish iced soup, which looks as good as it tastes. It needs to be very well chilled, so give it plenty of time to sit in the refrigerator (or serve it with an ice cube in the bottom of each soup bowl).

1½lb (675g) tomatoes, peeled	1 tablespoon wine vinegar
½ cucumber	salt, pepper
2 large cloves of garlic	cayenne pepper
12 black olives, stoned	chopped fresh marjoram or parsley
1 onion, finely chopped	
1 small green pepper, cut into strips	½ pint (¼l; 1 cup) iced water
3 or 4 tablespoons olive oil	1 thick slice brown wholemeal bread

Chop the tomatoes finely, until they are almost a pulp, add the diced unpeeled cucumber, the chopped garlic, olives, onion, green pepper, oil and vinegar, seasoning and herbs. You can make this into a smooth soup by putting it through a mouli at this stage, but it seems a pity to spoil its good looks and interesting texture. Chill this mixture and, just before serving, thin it down with iced water, and crumble in the bread. Hand round a bowl filled with roughly chopped cucumber, onion, olives, peppers and hard-boiled egg to sprinkle on top of the soup.

Provençal tomatoes

A delicious hot tomato hors d'oeuvre from the Mediterranean coast of France, where a meal without tomatoes would be almost unthinkable. Select large ripe tomatoes of approximately similar size, and cut them in half. Score and cut side with a sharp knife, and rub in salt, pepper and crushed garlic. Cover with chopped parsley and press well into the pulp. Sprinkle with olive oil and cook under a high flame until the tomatoes are slightly blackened.

Stuffed tomatoes

Tomatoes can be stuffed with practically anything, from leftovers to specially made fillings. Choose large firm tomatoes and cut a slice from the top of each. Scoop out the insides and remove the seeds by pushing the pulp through a sieve.

When baking tomatoes, it is best to get rid of as much moisture as possible. After cutting off the tops and carefully scooping out the pulp, put the tomatoes in a baking dish in the oven for just a few minutes. Remove them, and turn them upside down to drain. Season the shells and fill with stuffing. Put the tomatoes in a shallow dish with a little melted butter or oil, and baste them now and again so that they brown nicely. Stuffed tomatoes will need 20–40 minutes in a medium oven. If a recipe calls for breadcrumbs, they should first be moistened with a spoonful or two of stock. If you are going to use the pulp in the stuffing, reduce it first by cooking it quickly with a little butter.

Tomato ice (for 4)

3lb (1·35kg) ripe tomatoes	2 teaspoons tomato purée
1 small onion	pinch of sugar
1 teaspoon marjoram	juice of 1 small lemon

Peel and chop the skinned tomatoes and the onion, put them in a pan with the marjoram and simmer until the tomatoes are soft. Sieve into a large bowl and add the purée, sugar and lemon juice. Leave the mixture to cool before putting into a covered freezer container. Freeze overnight. Before serving, turn out the mixture and crush it into tiny crystals. Pile it into individual glass dishes and garnish with a sprig of mint or a few slices of cucumber. This makes an unusual starter.

Stuffed olive and anchovy tomatoes

6 large tomatoes	1 large clove of garlic
8 medium green olives	2oz (50g; ¼ cup) butter
2oz (50g; 2 cups) fresh white breadcrumbs	1 teaspoon basil or marjoram
6 anchovy fillets	

Make the stuffing with the scooped-out insides of the tomatoes (seeds removed), chopped garlic, chopped green olives, chopped anchovies, basil, fresh white breadcrumbs, melted butter and a little salt. Put the mixture back into the tomato halves and bake in the top of a warm oven (Reg 3/ 325°F) for 40 minutes until tender and brown.

Serve with a simple green salad.

Alternative hot fillings

Cooked rice, equal quantities of chopped onion and currants, garlic, pepper and salt, and a little left-over cooked lamb or beef. This is a Greek speciality, and the tomatoes should be cooked in a covered dish with olive oil.

Gruyère cheese melted in a double saucepan with black pepper, Dijon mustard, crushed garlic and cayenne pepper, moistened with white wine to give the mixture the consistency of thick cream. Bake in a moderate oven for about 10 minutes, then brown under a low flame.

Equal quantities of finely chopped cooked veal and moistened breadcrumbs, a little chopped onion that has been gently sweated in butter, garlic, a little tomato pulp and the yolk of an egg.

Equal quantities of breadcrumbs and chopped cooked chicken and ham, a finely chopped onion lightly browned in butter, and chopped mushrooms, also cooked in butter. Mix together with a bit of grated horseradish and some thickened chicken gravy.

Pour a raw egg into each tomato (keeping back some of the white, otherwise there will be no room for anything else). Blend the tomato pulp with cream and spoon the mixture over the eggs. Sprinkle with grated Parmesan cheese, and bake until the eggs have set.

Pound anchovy fillets with a little garlic, some drained tuna fish and herbs such as parsley, chives, chervil, tarragon, fennel and a small quantity of moistened breadcrumbs. Sprinkle with herbs before baking and serve on toast or fried bread.

Cold fillings

Diced cucumber, grated Cheddar cheese, mayonnaise, a few sprigs of cooked cauliflower, pepper, salt, paprika and a dash of Worcestershire sauce. Mix the tomato pulp with half the cucumber, the cheese, a little mayonnaise and seasoning. Spoon the mixture into the tomatoes and top up with the rest of the cucumber and mayonnaise and a sprig of cauliflower dusted with paprika.

Diced celery and apple with mayonnaise mixed with a little of the tomato pulp.

Tuna fish, finely grated onion, salt and a lot of freshly ground black pepper, mixed into a homemade mayonnaise.

Peeled prawns mixed with mayonnaise.

Cottage cheese, blended with thick cream and finely chopped chives, gherkin, garlic and fresh basil.

Thick cream, mayonnaise, lemon juice and grated horseradish mixed with a little tomato pulp. The mixture and the tomato shells should be chilled separately, and introduced to each other just before serving. Sprinkle with chopped basil.

Pasta dishes with tomatoes

Tomatoes and pasta were first introduced to each other in the sixteenth century, and the relationship has since gone from strength to strength. Traditionally, Marco Polo brought the secret of pasta-making to Italy on returning from his historic voyage to China. However they came by it, the Italians have taken pasta to their hearts, stuffing little parcels of it with the most remarkable fillings, flattening it out into fat wide ribbons, twisting it into delicate swirls, stamping out little stars, and, of course, drawing it out into long thin strands known as spaghetti. All the versions are eaten with tomato sauce.

In order to appreciate pasta, you have to cook it properly. Take the largest saucepan you have and fill it almost to the brim with water and a generous amount of salt. When, and only when the water is boiling furiously, throw the pasta into the pan and keep the water boiling. Do not cover the pan, and be careful not to overcook the pasta. Pasta is done when it reaches a critical stage somewhere between hard and soft – *al dente* they call it in Italy. (A chef once revealed his secret of testing for spaghetti's readiness: 'I fling a strand against the wall. If it sticks, it is done. If not, I cook it a bit longer.') The moment it is done, strain it, pile it into a heated serving dish with a knob of butter or a splosh of olive oil.

Tagliatelli with tomatoes and bacon

1lb (450g) tagliatelli (long, thin curled-up ribbons)	2 heaped tablespoons chopped cold roast pork
½lb (225g) mushrooms	1 clove of garlic, crushed
½lb (225g) tomatoes, peeled and chopped	parsley
	fresh basil leaves
2 rashers unsmoked bacon	salt, pepper
olive oil	grated Parmesan cheese

Slice the mushrooms, and cook them in oil over a low heat. Add the chopped-up bacon, the garlic and the tomatoes. Cook for 5 minutes, then add the cold pork, herbs and seasoning. Mix into the cooked and drained pasta, and stir in 1–2 tablespoons of Parmesan cheese.

Spaghetti with uncooked tomatoes

This easy, delicious dish needs a quantity of tomatoes, cut into thick slices. Allow them to sit for a while in olive oil, into which you have chopped some fresh basil leaves. As soon as the pasta is cooked and drained, mix it with the tomatoes, oil and herbs, and dish up at once: the contrast of the hot pasta and the cold tomatoes is the point of the dish. Hard-boiled eggs, coarsely chopped, and chopped boiled ham are sometimes mixed into the pasta together with the tomatoes.

Lasagne (*for 4–6*)

14–20 pieces lasagne	small cup stock
1 onion, finely chopped	salt, pepper
olive oil	2 cloves of garlic
¾lb (335g) minced pork and veal mixed	bay leaf
	2oz (50g; ½ cup) Gruyère cheese, grated
4 tomatoes, skinned and chopped	2oz (50g; ½ cup) grated Parmesan cheese
tomato purée	

Cook the lasagne in salted boiling water until just tender. Put each one in separately and keep moving. Sauté the onion in oil until just brown, add mince and fry, stirring until brown and crumbly. Add the tomatoes and tomato purée (add a little stock if too dry), salt, pepper, and crushed garlic. Cook for a good hour until smooth and rich. Make a Béchamel sauce and add the bay leaf and Gruyère cheese. Remove the bay leaf when smooth. Butter a gratin dish and arrange in it alternate layers of meat, sauce and lasagne: finish with the Béchamel. Sprinkle with Parmesan and cook in a moderate oven until golden brown.

Tomato salad

The tomatoes should come in contact with their dressing only at the very last moment. This way, they stay crisp and fresh. Dress them in a Vinaigrette with olives, in a *sauce verte* with plenty of basil, or – especially nice – in a garlic mayonnaise. (The liquid of the tomatoes will thin down the mayonnaise, but this is all to the good; the idea is to produce a barely bound, pinkish juice, to be scooped up with bread.

Spaghetti with cockles and tomato sauce

This is a favourite Roman dish, and should, ideally, be made with baby clams instead of cockles. For each person, buy 1 pint (½l; 4 cups) of cockles in their shells, or 2oz (50g) of cooked, shelled ones, from your fishmonger. To prepare cockles in their shells, wash them well, and leave them under running water to get rid of all the grit and sand. Put them, without water, into a pan, and shake them about over a high flame until the shells have opened. Strain, and remove the shells.

For 4 people, fry 1 chopped onion and 3 large cloves of garlic in oil. Add 6 large, peeled, chopped tomatoes. Let them bubble in the pan until they have been reduced slightly then add the cockles and a handful of chopped parsley. Heat through and pour the sauce over the spaghetti.

Italian tomato sauce (*for pasta, for 6*)

This sauce is the ordinary sauce of northern Italy, where it is made in a great batch once a week and eaten once or sometimes twice a day – not only with pasta, but also with polenta, pot-roasts, and even thick slices of toast.

Slice 1 large onion and chop 2 carrots and 1 stick of celery coarsely. Put them in a thick saucepan with 8 large skinned tomatoes, coarsely chopped. Add a few leaves of basil and simmer for 45 minutes, stirring the sauce from time to time, and adding a little water if it becomes dry, which is not likely. Add a little salt.

Turn the sauce out into a sieve, let the liquid run off and then sieve the sauce through the fine blade of a mouli-légumes. Return the sauce to the pan with 3 tablespoons of oil. Add 1 teaspoon of sugar if you feel it is needed.

Cold Greek tomatoes (*for 6*)

4 large tomatoes	12 black olives
1 lettuce (a Cos lettuce is ideal)	½ cucumber
	dressing of olive oil and lemon juice (or wine vinegar), salt and pepper
½lb (225g) fetta or other hard white cheese preferably goat's cheese	sprinkling of oregano

Simply break the fetta into small pieces that you can get on to a fork, wash the lettuce, dry it, break it in small pieces and put it into a wooden bowl. Cut the tomatoes into thickish slices. Cut the cucumber, lay it on the lettuce and arrange the tomatoes, cheese and olives on top. Sprinkle generous amounts of oregano over the whole. Sprinkle with olive oil.

Just before you eat the salad pour on the dressing, which should be rather plain, and turn it over well.

Baked tomatoes

Choose huge French tomatoes for baking. Green tomatoes

are also very good when baked, but need to be boiled first.

Put sliced skinned tomatoes on a buttered fireproof dish. Mix about 1 tablespoon of breadcrumbs with 2 tablespoons of finely chopped onion, some fresh basil and a crushed clove of garlic. Sprinkle over the tomatoes, dot with butter and bake, cut the skinned tomatoes in half and lay them in a buttered ovenproof dish. Dot with butter and sprinkle with salt, pepper, a little castor sugar and some finely chopped chervil and tarragon. Bake in a hot oven, basting occasionally, and serve with Béarnaise sauce.

Mix together equal quantities of skinned sliced tomatoes and cooked rice. Add about half an onion, finely chopped and cooked in butter, some fried aubergine or eggplant, and some mushrooms previously sautéed in butter. Season well and add grated Gruyère cheese. Dot with butter, and bake for at least 30 minutes.

Chinese steamed tomatoes (*for 6*)

Although this recipe has a rather daunting list of ingredients, it is a good way of using up irritatingly small leftovers.

2 heaped tablespoons chopped smoked ham	1 clove of garlic, crushed
2 heaped tablespoons chopped fish (haddock or cod)	1oz (25g; ⅛ cup) chicken fat
	6 large tomatoes
	vegetable oil
2 heaped tablespoons chopped cooked chicken	handful of cauliflower florets
4 or 5 mushrooms, chopped	½ cucumber, thickly sliced
1 slice of root ginger, finely chopped	stock
	salt
	cornflour

Pound the chicken, fish, ham, ginger, garlic and mushrooms – if you have them, use Chinese dried ones which have been soaked for 15 minutes – together with the chicken fat, to make a paste. Skin the tomatoes and slice off the tops, scooping out the pulp. Fill the tomato shells with the chicken and ham paste, and steam them and their lids in a heatproof dish for 15 minutes.

While the tomatoes are steaming, stir-fry the cauliflower and cucumber in hot vegetable oil for 2 minutes. Season with salt, add the stock and any left-over filling, stir well and let the mixture simmer for a further 2 minutes. Thicken with a couple of teaspoons of cornflour blended with cold water, and stir a little longer. To dish up, replace the lids on the tomatoes, arrange the cauliflower and cucumber around them, and pour the contents of the frying pan over the whole.

Tomato pie

In a buttered pie dish place alternate layers of sliced tomatoes – previously salted and drained – chopped ham, breadcrumbs and grated Parmesan cheese. Finish with a bread and cheese layer, pour melted butter over the whole, and bake.

Alternatively, leave out the ham, but then it is nice to line the dish with a thin layer of bacon. Whatever version –

and there is another with a central layer of onion rings softened in butter – dish it up topped with poached eggs.

Savoury tomato rice

Nice with lamb chops, chicken-livers and fried chicken joints. Cook rice in the usual quantity in the usual way. Before it is quite done, soften an onion in oil or butter in a deep pan, and add 1 chopped tomato for each person. Gently cook this sauce until you have a red mush. Strain it through a sieve straight on to the dry rice. Mix in well with a fork – a spoon would mash the grains to extinction – until the rice is the colour of a picture-postcard sunset.

Savoury tomato crumble

3 rashers back bacon	2oz (50g; ¼ cup) butter
2 onions	chopped parsley
6 slices wholemeal bread	chopped basil
1½lb (675g) tomatoes	salt, pepper; castor sugar

Cut the rind from the bacon, and finely chop up the rashers and the onions. Crumble the bread into the mixture, and add the herbs. Skin and thinly slice the tomatoes. In a shallow buttered ovenproof dish arrange alternate layers of the crumb mixture and sliced tomatoes, seasoning the tomatoes with salt, pepper and sugar as you go. Finish off with a layer of crumbs, dot with butter and bake in a fairly hot oven for about 30 minutes until the crumble is brown and bubbling.

Tomato mousse

6 large tomatoes	salt
1oz (25g; ⅛ cup) butter	freshly ground black pepper
1 spring onion, chopped	1 clove
3 or 4 mushrooms, chopped	2 level tablespoons gelatine
tarragon leaves	per pint (½l) of purée
1 teaspoon sugar	3 tablespoons cream,
1 pinch bicarbonate of soda	whipped

Skin the tomatoes, halve them and press out the seeds. Cut them up and simmer in butter until tender with the onion, mushrooms, tarragon leaves, sugar, bicarbonate of soda, clove, salt and pepper. Take out the clove and sieve the mixture into a basin. Check the seasoning and add the gelatine dissolved in water. When it looks as if the tomato is beginning to set, add the stiffly whipped cream, mix well, pour into a wetted mould and chill. Serve with a green salad. or a green vegetable salad to enhance the colour of the mousse.

Tomatoes on toast

Peel and roughly chop 2 or 3 tomatoes per person. Simmer them in a covered pan with a generous lump of butter, salt, a pinch of sugar, pepper, and a dash of Worcestershire sauce. Serve on hot buttered toast and eat immediately.

Tomato fondue

Stew tomatoes as in the previous recipe and add a pinch of

Zucchini
Cucurbita pepo

bicarbonate of soda. Mix with an equal quantity of Bechamel sauce and some grated Gruyere cheese. Stir until the cheese has melted, then let the tomatoes cool slightly before adding 1 egg yolk for each ½ pint (¼l; 1 cup) of mixture. Serve quickly on hot buttered toast.

Tomato purée

Skin the tomatoes, cut them in halves and press out the seeds. Chop them up and simmer in a covered pan with a small, finely chopped onion, a bouquet garni and a little sugar. Remove the bouquet, and sieve the tomato mixture. Return the mixture to a clean pan and simmer slowly until the purée thickens. Season with salt and pepper only when it reaches the consistency you want, as, although tomatoes may evaporate, salt does not, and well-flavoured tomato pulp could turn into a very salty tomato purée.

Mexican tomato sauce

In Mexico this hot sauce is as common as the commercially made ketchup which graces our tables. Chop up 2 large ripe tomatoes which have been skinned, 2 hot green chillies, 1 small onion and some fresh coriander leaves. Mix and season with salt, black pepper and a little castor sugar.

VEGETABLE MARROWS AND ZUCCHINI
Cucurbita pepo

The European marrows – called courgettes in France,

zucchini in Italy – are called squash in the USA. The rind and seed of this plant, also called the pumpkin, have been discovered in South and Central American tombs dating back to 2000 BC; and the word squash itself comes from its aboriginal name. No one can say much about its European origins. Marrow flowers – regarded as a fertility symbol by some Indian tribes – were certainly eaten as sweet fritters by medieval Englishmen, who used to spice them with cinnamon and ginger, rather as the Italians do to this day. Unlike Mediterranean zucchini-eaters, however, even twentieth-century Englishmen used to grow marrows to gargantuan harvest-festival sizes before bringing them into the kitchen, deaf to the reports of seventeenth-century travellers who liked the look and taste of small ones. Luckily we no longer feel any qualms about eating infant and baby marrows, which are as delicious as the monster marrows are inedible. Old or young, marrows contain a trace of vitamins B and C, and very few calories, which makes them a boon to slimmers.

Basic treatment

Whether you are dealing with marrow or zucchini, trim at both ends, and, in most cases, wipe the outside and do not peel. (Only in the case of diced, cooked vegetable marrow would you go so far as to peel it.) Boiling, steaming, frying and baking times vary, but will not be less than 15 minutes, or more than 1 hour, for a baked stuffed giant (provided it has been parboiled before going into the oven).

Spanish vegetable soup (*for 4–6*)

½lb (225g) zucchini	2 teaspoons sweet ground
2 large potatoes	pimento (paprika will do)
1 large clove of garlic	1lb (450g) tomatoes
2 medium-sized or 1 large	2 pints (1¼l; 4 cups) stock
onion	1 teaspoon dried basil
3 tablespoons oil	salt, pepper

Cut the zucchini into small rounds, the potatoes into cubes and the garlic into slivers. Chop the onions and put them in a pan with the olive oil. Let them soften over a gentle heat. Add the cut-up vegetables to the onions. Stir in the pimento and let everything soften while you skin the tomatoes and chop them. Add them to the other vegetables, and let them simmer for 10 minutes before adding the stock and basil.

Let the soup boil for 30 minutes or more, covered with a tilted lid – the fast boiling is important to blend the ingredients – and taste it for seasoning. If the tomatoes have not seen much sun, you may need to add a lump of sugar.

It is a fairly thick soup, almost a stew, rich red with little green rounds of zucchini just visible. In the summer you can add a handful of green beans about 20 minutes before you want to serve the soup.

Frittata of zucchini (*for 6*)

1lb (450g) zucchini	salt
2–3 tablespoons olive oil	pepper
or a lump of butter	1 small onion, chopped and
1 heaped tablespoon fresh	sautéed for a few minutes
breadcrumbs	in butter
1 heaped tablespoon grated	6 eggs
Parmesan cheese	

Slice the zucchini into little rounds about ¼in (½cm) thick and soften them in oil or butter in a shallow pan over gentle heat for 15 minutes. If you are going to eat this dish hot, use butter; if cold, use oil.

Mix the breadcrumbs, cheese, zucchini, salt and pepper in a bowl. Stir in the partly cooked onion. Beat the eggs lightly and stir into the courgette mixture.

Heat the oil (or butter) in a large frying pan, turn the zucchini mixture into it and when the underneath is set and slightly browned, sprinkle the top with more cheese, and push the pan under a high flame. When the mixture is a good deep golden colour, remove it and eat it hot or cold, cut into wedges.

Stuffed zucchini (*for 6 as a starter; for 4 as a vegetable*)

6 medium-sized zucchini	oregano
1 small onion	½ pint (¼l; 1 cup) chicken
1 tablespoon butter	stock
2 tablespoons pine nuts	2 tablespoons oil
1 tablespoon long-grain	salt, pepper
rice	1 mashed clove of garlic

Preheat the oven to Reg 4/350°F. Halve the zucchini lengthways and, with a small pointed knife, scoop out the middles, which you keep on one side for the stuffing. Chop the onion finely, sauté it in butter in a sauté pan or saucepan, without browning, until tender and transparent. Add the pine nuts and continue cooking for 4–5 minutes.

Add the rice and cook gently, stirring, for 3 minutes more. Add the chopped flesh from the zucchini, the garlic and a large pinch of oregano. Pour on the boiling stock, season with salt and pepper and simmer, covered for 10–15 minutes until the rice is tender. Add more stock if necessary. The mixture should end up fairly dry but holding together.

Meanwhile gently sauté the zucchini halves in oil until they start to soften. Fill them with the pine-nut mixture and arrange them in a buttered gratin dish. Cover with foil and bake for 40 minutes. Serve with a lemon sauce.

Casseroled zucchini (*for 4*)

4 medium-sized zucchini	2 eggs, lightly beaten
1 tablespoon butter	2 tablespoons grated
1½ cups cold Béchamel	Parmesan cheese
sauce	salt, pepper

Slice the zucchini and fry in butter until light brown, taking care not to overcook. Mix together the sauce, eggs, Parmesan, salt and pepper, and fold in the fried zucchini.

Butter and flour a casserole, pour in the zucchini mixture and place the uncovered casserole in a pan of water in a moderate oven (Reg 4/350°F) for 45 minutes to 1 hour.

Let it stand for 5 minutes after removing it from the oven and before turning out on to a serving dish.

Baked zucchini with rice (*for 4–6*)

Peel and slice 4 zucchini. Peel and chop 1 onion, and gently fry both in olive oil in which 1 clove of garlic has been crushed. Add about 5 heaped tablespoons of cooked rice and 1 large skinned tomato. Simmer for about 5 minutes. Turn the mixture into a fireproof dish, moisten with a glass of white wine, cover with grated cheese and brown in the oven.

Zucchini salad (*for 2–4*)

1lb (450g) small zucchini	salt, pepper
juice of ½ lemon	sugar
6 tablespoons olive oil	chopped parsley

Boil the whole zucchini in salted water until they are just done. While they are cooking, make a dressing with the lemon juice, olive oil, sugar and seasoning, and slice the hot zucchini into it. Chill and serve with a handful of parsley.

Vegetable marrow and tomato

Cut the peeled marrow into cubes and boil it briskly in salted water until it is tender and transparent. Meanwhile, in another pan, soften some chopped onions in oil or butter,

add a few cut-up skinned tomatoes, stir, and cook over medium heat until you have a fragrant gooey sauce. Just before you are ready to dish up, add the drained marrow to the tomato. Serve hot. This takes about 20 minutes to make.

In another version, which takes longer but is superior in so far as both vegetables cook in their own juice, the cubed marrow and sliced tomatoes go into a casserole (with a well-fitting lid) in alternate layers, with the addition of a few onion rings. A layer of marrow, dotted with butter, forms the top. Cover the casserole with the lid, and cook in the centre of a moderate oven for about 3 hours.

Marrow flower fritters

These are made with the large, beautiful golden flowers which makes marrows such an asset in flower-beds as well as in the kitchen garden. Since the zucchini or marrow grows from the stem of the flower, it is not robbing Peter to pay Paul to remove the flower once the vegetable has started to form. Anyway, they bloom and fruit so profusely that it is sometimes a good idea to thin them out a bit, particularly zucchini, which become too large, it seems, overnight.

Stuff each flower with a mixture of breadcrumbs, chopped onions, fried but not browned, egg yolk, parsley and grated lemon rind. Dip it in batter, shaking off the surplus before deep frying.

For the batter you will need 4oz (110g; 1 cup) flour; salt; a knob of butter, melted; $\frac{1}{4}$ pint ($\frac{3}{8}$l) light ale; 1 egg white. Sieve the flour and salt into a bowl. Make a well in the

centre and pour in the just-melted butter. Start incorporating the flour and gradually add the ale. When you have a smooth thickish mixture, the consistency of thick cream, let it stand for about 1 hour. When you are just about to use it, beat the egg white to stiff peaks and add it to the mixture, folding it in until it is well incorporated. This batter should give a smooth, crisp, delicate coating.

Deep-fry to a golden crust and drain well on absorbent paper before serving.

Stuffed vegetable marrow

Cut a good-sized marrow lengthways and scoop out the seeds until you have two primitive boats. Parboil for 10 minutes in salted water. (If your marrow is too gigantic to fit into even your largest vessel, stand the halves up in the pan and boil them in two shifts, as it were, by turning them top to bottom after 10 minutes are up. It does not matter if the middle sections are given two cookings.) Then remove the marrow from the water.

For the stuffing, mince about 4oz (110g; 1 cup) fresh or cooked minced meat, 4 tablespoons cooked rice, 3 chopped onions previously softened in oil, herbs and seasoning, with 2 eggs. Spoon this mixture into the cavity of one of the marrow halves, and cover it with the other. Bake in a greased baking dish in a slowish oven for $1\frac{1}{2}$ hours, or until soft.

Serve in slices cut as though you are slicing bread. Make sure you have a sharp, large, possibly a saw-toothed, knife for this operation – the skin of old marrows can be very hard.

How to grow marrows, pumpkins, cucumbers

The vegetable marrow comes in several types, trailing and bush, and is plain green or striped or cream. The bush varieties are usually more prolific and, of course, take up less room in the garden. They need soil with a lot of moisture and a sunny, sheltered position. Well-rotted compost should be dug into the site in winter. The seeds are sown *in situ* in late spring under glass, or in small pots under glass and hardened off before planting in early spring A little more compost dug in first is a good idea. Give bush types about 4ft (1·20m) area and trailers 6ft (1·80m). Cut and eat the marrows when they are young and tender; really small ones are delicious skin and all. The more you cut the more will grow. Water well in dry weather as these plants need plenty of moisture. Prick two or three times a week until the end of summer. Pumpkins are worth growing if you have plenty of room. The seeds are sown like those of the marrow. There are two main types of cucumber; those for growing in greenhouses or in frames under glass which are long and smooth; and those grown outside, called ridge cucumbers, which are shorter and prickly skinned. Ridge cucumbers are sown in the open in early summer. They need about 3ft (90cm) space each way as they tend to spread themselves. Indoor or glasshouse cucumbers need to be sown in spring in warmth. They need a well-dug, rich soil, but no disturbance round their roots; and care must be taken not to let the stems get wet when watering, as they may rot. If you feel up to it, the male flowers should be removed from greenhouse cucumbers; if they are left the fruit can taste bitter. (Female flowers have a small bulge in the stem.) Fruit under glass may also need shading from the sun. Always cut before the fruits are too old.

1. Dig compost into soil; marrows and pumpkins are greedy feeders

2. Put the seeds in pots under glass, or outside under jam jars

3. Water well in dry weather, plants must not dry out

4. Pick small and tender, allowing a few to become huge for the winter

Pumpkin soup with lovage

Pumpkins left over from Hallowe'en make a good basis for this soup, to which lovage adds an exotic taste rather like a mixture of celery and curry.

2 onions	$\frac{1}{4}$ pumpkin
garlic if liked	2 pints ($1\frac{1}{4}$l; 4 cups) stock
1 tablespoon butter or olive oil	salt
	$\frac{1}{2}$ pint ($\frac{1}{4}$l; 1 cup) milk
2 tablespoons lovage	2 tablespoons chopped
1 heaped tablespoon flour	parsley

Slice the onions and crush the garlic, and sauté in the butter. Add the lovage, then the flour, and cook for a few minutes. Add the pumpkin, diced, the stock and salt. Stir until it comes to the boil, then simmer until the pumpkin is cooked. Add the milk, and put through a sieve or mouli, or whizz for an instant in the blender. Gently reheat and add chopped parsley before serving. Serve with croûtons and a little bowl of crushed, crisply fried bacon.

CUCUMBER *Cucumis sativus*

Like the rest of the cucurbitacea, cucumbers date back for thousands of years. The Chinese enjoyed them; the Israelites grieved over the lack of them in the desert; the Romans cultivated them in heat and used them all the year round; Charlemagne grew them in his herbal garden and listed them in his great botanical book; Columbus found them in Haiti, and they were later discovered in places as far apart as Montreal and Florida.

Raw cucumbers, however, were thought by sixteenth-century Europeans to cause trouble. Their juice, it was said, easily corrupted in human veins, although they were recommended 'as meate for mules and asses'.

Cooked cucumbers were quite a different proposition: taken for 3 weeks without a break (though with additions of oatmeal, mutton and herbs) they would cure, said Gerard, 'all manner of phlegm, and copper faces, red and shining fiery noses and every sort of pimple and pumple'. The face being washed with their juice, said a later authority, 'cureth all rednesse'; and cucumber juice and jelly is said to be a potent ingredient of some twentieth-century 'nature' cosmetics.

It was, in fact, only in the twentieth century that raw cucumbers came into their own – both Mrs Acton and Mrs Beeton confined themselves to cooking and pickling 'cow-cumbers'; though by the middle of the nineteenth century 'only people of the old school' still used this archaic word.

Cucumbers do not contain much by way of nutrients, though they have a certain amount of Vitamin C.

Basic treatment

To cook them, peel, cut and sweat them in salt first to get rid of excess liquid. For salads, only old specimens need peeling

– commercial growers have bred the skin of the cucumber so thin that it is perfectly digestible.

Cucumber soup (*for 4*)

1 small cucumber, peeled
1 medium-sized potato, peeled
4–5 spring onions
butter

2 pints (1¼l; 4 cups) good chicken stock
salt and freshly ground pepper

Grate the cucumber and potato coarsely; strain off the liquid that forms and put the vegetables to sweat with the finely chopped onions in enough butter to cover the bottom of a medium saucepan. Heat the stock to simmering point and add to the vegetables. Simmer gently for 20–25 minutes. Check the seasoning and serve with a knob of butter in each bowl.

Boiled cucumbers

Reckon ½ cucumber and 4 tablespoons of Béchamel sauce per person. Cook the cucumbers, cut into 1in (2·5cm) cubes, in salted water for 5–10 minutes. Drain and set aside. Heat the Bechamel sauce, adding the cucumber dice when it is hot. Stirring steadily over gentle heat, add 2 tablespoons of butter, very gradually, in minute quantities. When all is smooth and integrated, dish up at once.

Poached cucumber

Peel 3 cucumbers and cut them into chunks about 3in (7·5cm) long. Poach them in salted water until tender. Drain well and put into a shallow dish. Keep hot. Mix the yolk of 1 egg with 6 tablespoons of sour cream to make a pale yellow sauce. Warm this sauce (without letting it boil) by beating it in a bowl set over hot water. Spread it over the cucumbers, generously sprinkle with chopped dill and chives – more dill than chives – and eat with black bread and butter.

Hot cucumbers

2 cucumbers
2oz (50g; ¼ cup) butter
2oz (50g; ½ cup) flour
½ pint (¼l; 1 cup) milk

2 tablespoons chopped chives
salt
pepper

Cut the cucumbers into cubes, leaving the skin on, put them into boiling water and cook for 5 minutes. Drain. Make a white sauce with the butter, flour and milk, and stir in the cucumbers, chives, salt and pepper.

This is nice enough to serve as a separate course, but delicious with fish or meat.

German cucumber salads

Finely slice the cucumber – a mandoline is best for this purpose, as the slices should be so thin as to be transparent.

Cucumber
Cucumis sativus

Cover with sour cream, or cream soured by the addition of a dash of white wine vinegar. Sprinkle with chopped chives, or some of the green part of a spring onion (scallion), or even the green part of a leek, finely chopped – a slight flavour of onion is essential.

In Austria, where *Gurkensalat* is the inevitable accompaniment to the ubiquitous *Bachändl*, cucumbers are first sliced to film-like thinness, and then sprinkled with salt, which draws out the liquid and makes the cucumbers soft. Then the salad is dressed with oil, vinegar or lemon, and dished up sprinkled with paprika.

Cucumber and melon salad

Peel a well-chilled cucumber. Scoop out the flesh from half an equally cold honeydew melon, and cut both into dice. Dress in a mixture of thin cream, lemon juice, salt, a good pinch of sugar and a shiff of curry powder. Serve at once, while the salad is still icy cold, and before the cubes have had a chance to render too much of their juices. Even so, it is an hors d'oeuvre best eaten with a spoon. Chopped mint is sometimes added.

Hungarian cucumber salad

Dice the peeled cucumber – the cubes should be about the size of large peas. Mix with 1 generous teaspoon of chopped onion, and add as much yoghourt as is needed to allow the cucumber to be well covered. To each tablespoonful of diced cucumber, there should be at least one of yoghourt. Cover, and put in the refrigerator for 1 hour before it is needed – it should be well chilled, and is extremely refreshing.

Turkish salad

1 cucumber	$\frac{3}{4}$ pint ($\frac{1}{2}$l; 1$\frac{1}{2}$ cups)
salt, pepper	yoghourt
1–2 cloves of garlic	3 tablespoons chopped mint

Slice or dice the cucumber (with the skin on) and leave it, salted, in a colander for 30 minutes to drain. Crush the garlic with salt or squeeze it in a garlic crusher (if you like it, use 3 cloves), mix it well with the yoghourt and season it. Add the pepper, the chopped mint and finally the drained cucumber pieces. Serve with an extra sprinkling of mint.

PEPPER *Capsicum frutescens*

Sweet peppers, or pimentos, are members of the chilli family, which comes in all shapes and sizes, and as far as taste is concerned, runs the gamut from the bland to the murderously hot. As a rule of thumb, the larger the pepper the cooler its taste, though even sweet peppers were found to be 'full of peppers which burn the mouth' by an aggrieved sixteenth-century European cultivator. Soon after Columbus had brought this interesting new vegetable back from his travels, its cultivation spread all over Europe. Many pimento dishes are traditionally called *à l'espagnole*; and the trademark of Hungarian cookery is paprika, which is made from pimento – but peppers also appear in dishes called *à la créole*, *à la turque* and *à la russienne*, so far-flung is its geography.

Sweet peppers contain vitamins A and C, and some vitamin B1.

Basic treatment

It is wise to de-seed peppers properly – the little peppercorns can be exceedingly hot. So remove the core by carefully scooping it out. If a recipe calls for peppers halved or chopped, you will be able to see what you are doing, but if they must be kept whole – as for stuffed peppers – remove the core, together with the stalk, and then wash out the pepper as you would a cup; this will dislodge any seeds that have escaped you. Drain, upside down, before stuffing. For any dish needing peeled peppers, they are best charred under a flame or over gentle heat. This not only lets the skin come off easily, but makes the peppers more succulent and sweet-tasting.

Peperonata (*for 6*)

The Italians call the pepper *peperone*, and use them for this quick and easy stew.

6 large peppers	garlic
2 onions	3 tablespoons oil
6 tomatoes	salt

Cut the peppers into strips, chop the onion and tomato, and crush the garlic. In a covered pan, simmer the peppers and onions over a very gentle heat in the oil, to which the garlic has been added. When they are softened – but not browned – add the tomatoes, stirring occasionally so that nothing clings to the bottom of the pan. After the tomatoes have yielded their juice, finish cooking without replacing the lid. This stew can be eaten hot or cold.

Sweet peppers à la vinaigrette

Slice sweet peppers finely and, unless you want them very crunchy, marinate them in a good salad dressing for an hour or so before use. Garnish with thin, transparent onion rings and chopped hard-boiled eggs sprinkled over the top.

Red peppers with spinach (*for 4*)

2 red peppers	2 cloves of garlic
2lb (900g) spinach	salt
olive oil	pepper

Cut the cored peppers into quarters. Drop into boiling salted water to which you have added a spoonful of oil. Let them cook until tender, about 10 minutes, then drain.

Wash, cook and drain the spinach. Squeeze it in your hands to extract the water, then heat a little olive oil in a sauté pan and add the spinach with the chopped garlic, salt and pepper. Stir well and cook gently for about 10 minutes.

Arrange in a shallow dish, peppers in the centre, spinach round the edge. Serve with lamb or veal.

Sweet peppers and tomato stew (*to eat with sausages*)

De-seed 3 peppers and cut them into strips. Fry them gently in oil in a covered pan for about 10 minutes with a chopped clove of garlic and skinned, roughly chopped tomatoes. Cook until you have a red combined mixture, something between a sauce and a vegetable purée. Fresh chopped basil is a nice final touch.

Peppers and tuna fish hors d'oeuvre

2 peppers	olive oil
2 tomatoes	lemon juice
tuna fish	black olives

Broil or grill the peppers under strong heat until they are black and charred. Rub and rinse off the burned skin under the tap. Then halve and remove the core, cutting the flesh into broad strips short enough to be forked easily by the diners. Slice the tomatoes, flake the fish, dress with olive oil and lemon juice. Arrange a few black olives on top.

Pepper
Capsicum frutescens

Pepper and tomato salpicon

Peppers and tomatoes are perfect with pork or lamb chops. First fry the meat in hot fat, then lift out and keep warm. Sweat a chopped onion in the fat and juices. Add a sliced, de-seeded green pepper, stir, and simmer on a low heat. Skin 6 good-sized tomatoes, chop them roughly, and add them to the contents of the pan. Cook for another 10 minutes, season with salt, a few grains of sugar and a drop or two of lemon juice, and spoon over the chops.

Piperade

Left-over *ratatouille*, or newly stewed peppers, onion and aubergines are transformed into this Basque dish by the addition of an egg mixture. Allow 1 egg per person, and about 1 half-shell of milk. Beat well, more briskly than you would for scrambled eggs. Hurl into the gently bubbling vegetables and stir well until the web of cooked egg becomes an integral part of the mixture.

Neapolitan stuffed peppers

4 large peppers	1 tablespoon chopped basil
8 tablespoons olive oil	1 tablespoon chopped parsley
breadcrumbs	2 tablespoons capers
3 tablespoons raisins	salt,
12 black olives, pitted and cut into pieces	pepper
	4 tablespoons olive oil
6 anchovy fillets, chopped	4 tablespoons tomato sauce

Wash the peppers thoroughly. Remove the cores, leaving an opening through which stuffing may be pushed.

Mix together 8 tablespoons olive oil, breadcrumbs, raisins, olives, anchovies, parsley, basil, capers, salt and pepper. Mix well and if stuffing seems too dry, add more oil.

Stuff the peppers and place them standing up in a deep baking dish. Pour oil over the peppers and top each with 1 tablespoon of tomato sauce. Bake in a moderate oven (Reg 4/350°F) for 1 hour. This dish can be served either hot or cold.

The stuffing for the peppers can obviously be varied: chopped meat, diced bacon, chicken livers, ham, mushrooms or chopped hard-boiled eggs, or combinations of any of these, can be substituted for anchovies, and cooked rice can take the place of breadcrumbs. To mix a raw beaten egg into the stuffing will lighten it, binding the stuffing with egg yolk, and folding a whipped white of egg into it, will make it rise and give you a sort of soufflé.

Pimento butter (*delicious on brown bread*)

4oz (110g; ½ cup) butter	¼ clove garlic
2 small red peppers, finely chopped	juice of ½ lemon
	salt, pepper

Beat together thoroughly all the ingredients, pot and store.

Vegetable pulao (*for 4–6*)

½lb (225g) long-grain rice	½lb (225g) green beans
1 onion	2 carrots
2 tablespoons melted butter or oil	½lb (225g) cabbage
	2 tomatoes
¼ teaspoon cummin seeds	3 green peppers
4 cardamoms	½ teaspoon salt
2 cloves of garlic	

You can add a number of different vegetables to this rice but perhaps the best selection is onions, garlic, green peppers, carrots, green beans and walnuts. You can also add cauliflower, mushrooms, peas, cabbage, almonds, even ham or chicken if you like, but not too many things at once. This is a simple family recipe from Delhi.

Soak rice for 30 minutes in cold water. Drain, drop it

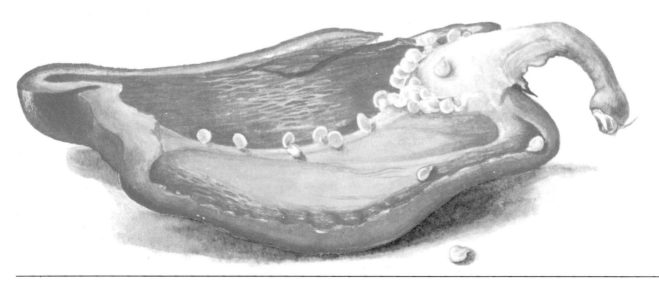

into plenty of boiling salted water and cook for 8–10 minutes until tender but with a bite. Drain off the extra water, cover the pan and stand it over a very low heat for 5–10 minutes when the rice will have dried and finished cooking. Meanwhile, slice the onion finely and soften it in the butter, together with the cummin and cardamom seeds and sliced garlic. When they start to brown, add the beans and the carrots cut up fairly small and ½ teaspoon of salt, and fry for 2–3 minutes, stirring to prevent them from cooking unevenly. Add the cabbage, cut up small, the green peppers, some freshly ground black pepper, and the chopped tomatoes. Then add the cooked rice, loosening it with a fork. Stir until it is well mixed with the vegetables, and add chopped walnuts or almonds if you like.

Stir and serve. This pulao is very good with Tandoori chicken, or any meat curry.

Red pepper, chicory and rice salad (for 3–4)

De-seed and skin 2 red peppers; dice the flesh. Mix with ½lb (225g) cooked rice and a chopped-up head of chicory in a good Vinaigrette. Some coarsely chopped walnuts can be added; they make a nice contrast in texture.

AUBERGINE *Solanum melongena*

Aubergines, also called egg-plants because of a pure white variety shaped like the egg of an enormous goose, graduated from being Gerard's 'madde or raging apple with a mischievous quality, the use whereof is utterly to be forsaken' to 'the choicest kind of annual' of the eighteenth century. Although this vegetable originates in warm countries, it will grow and yield in cooler climates.

Basic treatment

Before aubergines are cooked, they should be made to yield their excess liquid. This is done by making them sweat. Cover their cut surfaces with salt about 1 hour before they are to be used (if they are halved, prick their flesh with a fork to allow the salt to penetrate). Then rinse well, wipe dry, and proceed according to the recipe. Aubergines destined for cooking in their entirety do not, of course, need to be drained.

Turkish aubergines (1)

Aubergines often feature in Turkish cookery, and appear with any number of fragrant stuffings. They are eaten both hot and cold. The first version given here is called Imam Baldi – 'the Imam has fainted' – because, traditionally, that is just what he did from sheer joy when presented with this dish.

Halve the unpeeled vegetables lengthways, and take out the pulp, leaving a finger-thick wall of flesh. Prepare the stuffing by mixing the pulp with chopped onion, tomatoes and currants plumped up in a little water. Fry this mixture in oil for 3 or 4 minutes, and spoon it into the aubergines. Then

How to grow peppers and aubergines

Capsicums and sweet peppers are easy and rewarding to grow. Seed is sown under glass in early spring and plants are pricked off into pots. In a greenhouse or on a sunny window-sill they will give you early crops and also look very decorative (they were, after all, grown by the Victorians before tomatoes became fashionable). In warmer areas they do well in a sheltered border outside. Green peppers are the red fruits picked before they change colour.

Red chillies (cayenne pepper) are grown in the same way as peppers. They can be strung up in a dry place and stored for flavouring in the winter.

Aubergines need a temperature of 60°F (15°C) to start them off. Sow the seed in boxes and after 3 or 4 weeks pot the seedlings in small pots. They can then be planted in a greenhouse bed, outside in a sheltered, warm position, or under glass. Pinch out the growing plants and allow only 6 or 7 fruits per plant. Keep moist, or the glossy skin will split. From an early spring sowing you should be able to eat them in late summer.

1. Peppers are sown in boxes under glass and pricked out into pots

2. When they have grown into sturdy plants, they can be transplanted into the open

put the vegetables side by side in a dish, and cover them with oil, a bay leaf, some thyme and tarragon. Cook for 2 hours over a low heat, allow to cool in the oil, then drain and chill very well.

Turkish aubergines (2)

As above, remove the pulp from aubergine halves, chop and mix it, with a little cooked rice, some finely chopped cooked mutton, garlic, parsley and seasoning. Fry gently in oil, spoon the mixture into the cavities, strew with grated cheese and dot with butter. Cook in a slow oven until brown and tender. Eat with tomato sauce or without it.

Aubergine fritters (for 6–8)

4 large aubergines	deep oil for frying
salt	fritter batter

Cut the aubergines in slices, lengthways, drain, wash and dry the slices, and coat with batter. Heat the oil in a deep pan and deep-fry the aubergines to a golden brown. Drain very well before serving. These fritters are excellent with lamb.

Aubergine
Solanum melongena

Skewers Neapolitan style (*for 4*)

1 medium-sized aubergine	$\frac{1}{2}$ teaspoon salt
8 small tomatoes	$\frac{1}{4}$ teaspoon pepper
$\frac{3}{4}$lb (335g) mozzarella cheese	$\frac{1}{4}$ pint ($\frac{1}{8}$l; $\frac{1}{2}$ cup) milk
16 slices French bread (long loaf)	4oz (110g) flour
	2 eggs lightly beaten
	$\frac{1}{2}$ pint ($\frac{1}{4}$l; 1 cup) oil

Peel the aubergine and cut into $\frac{1}{2}$in (1cm) slices. Cut each slice in half. Peel the tomatoes, cut off the tops, drain off the juice and cut in two. Cut the mozzarella in slices about as large as aubergine slices. Have 8 skewers ready. Start each skewer with a slice of bread, then aubergine, mozzarella, half tomato, the aubergine, and so on, until the skewer is filled, ending with a bread slice. Sprinkle with a little salt and pepper, dip the skewers in milk, roll in flour and dip into egg. Deep-fry in hot oil until golden brown on both sides.

These are extremely rich, good and filling. Serve them with a green salad.

Melanzana Parmigiana (*for 6*)

3lb (1$\frac{1}{2}$kg) aubergines	Parmesan cheese, grated
salt	$\frac{1}{2}$lb (225g) mozzarella cheese
olive oil	
homemade tomato sauce	knob of butter

Slice the aubergines lengthways and sprinkle them with salt. Put them in a colander to drain with a heavy plate on top.

Rinse the drained aubergines, pat them dry and fry them on both sides in olive oil, adding more oil as it is needed. When they are brown, drain them, on absorbent paper.

When they are all fried, put a layer of aubergines in a large oval gratin dish, cover with well-seasoned tomato sauce and sprinkle with grated Parmesan cheese. Repeat the layers until all the aubergines are used up, ending with a layer of tomato sauce. Slice the mozzarella and arrange a layer of slices over the whole. Dot with butter and bake in a warm oven (Reg 3/325°F) for 1 hour. If it is not browned on top, put it under heat until the mozzarella is glazed and golden, but not for too long or it will become dry and rubbery.

Poor man's caviar

Put a large aubergine in the hot ashes of a wood fire, leave it there for about 1 hour, occasionally heaping on more ashes.

When split open, and scooped out, the inside of the aubergine has something of the texture of caviar but, sadly not its heady flavour.

Moussaka

Aubergines are a traditional part of this dish. Zucchini may be used too, either as an alternative or mixed with aubergines.

4 or 5 aubergines or zucchini (or a mixture)	cinnamon
oil	salt, pepper
2 onions, chopped finely	1lb (450g) tomatoes
garlic	tomato purée
1½lb (675g) lamb or beef, minced	3–4 tablespoons chopped marjoram
1 teaspoon allspice or	red wine or water

Fry the sliced aubergines/zucchini lightly in oil; put them to dry on kitchen paper. Fry the sliced onions with a little garlic until golden, add the meat and fry until brown. Add the spices, seasoning, tomatoes, some tomato purée and the marjoram. Stir well, add a little water (or better, red wine), and cook for 20 minutes. Put alternate layers of the meat mixture and the vegetables in a deep baking dish. Make a Béchamel sauce and add an egg yolk. Pour the sauce over the meat and vegetables and bake in a moderate oven (Reg 4/350°F) for about 45 minutes.

Ratatouille

¼ pint (⅛l; ½ cup) olive oil	3 cloves of garlic
2lb (900g) tomatoes	2 red peppers or, failing this, green
salt, pepper	
sugar	1lb (450g) zucchini
2–3 onions	1 large aubergine

Ratatouille comes from the south of France, where it varies from a delicate mixture of lightly cooked vegetables to a really dark brown stew, floating with oil and exuding garlic.

Ideally it should be a rich moist dish with different vegetables just distinguishable in a smooth, aromatic tomato sauce. Frying the vegetables with the tomatoes helps them to remain themselves.

Heat 6 tablespoons olive oil in a small pan. Skin the tomatoes and chop them. Simmer them in the oil with a seasoning of salt, pepper and 2 good pinches of sugar for 10–15 minutes.

Meanwhile, heat 6 tablespoons of oil in a heavy-bottomed pan and throw in the onions, sliced fairly coarsely downwards. Slice in 3 cloves of garlic and let it fry gently. Cut up the peppers into strips or squares and when the onions are soft throw these in, then the zucchini cut into thickish slices or quartered lengthways, and finally the aubergine cut in slices and then quartered. Add salt and continue to cook slowly.

When these vegetables are shining and beginning to soften, add the tomatoes which will be a fairly moist sauce. This will absorb all the oil. Gently stir the vegetables round quite often at all stages of cooking this dish, otherwise they will cook unevenly and stick to the bottom of the pan.

When all the vegetables are soft and tender the ratatouille is done. You can add thyme, or black olives, or more garlic to your ratatouille to change it. It reheats very well but can also be eaten cold as a summer salad-lunch.

Stuffed aubergines (*for 6*)

3 aubergines	2 teaspoons sugar
4 tablespoons white breadcrumbs	salt
	pepper

Cut the aubergines lengthways, scrape out the pulp, chop, and mix with the crumbs and the sugar, salt and pepper. Spoon this mixture back into the halved shells until they are well filled. Sprinkle each mound with 1 tablespoon of water, top with a knob of butter, and cook in a slow oven for 30 minutes.

Aubergine pie

6 aubergines	6oz (160g) hard cheese, sliced
6 tomatoes	
1 onion	3 tablespoons hard cheese, grated
oil	
flour	salt, pepper
3 sliced hard-boiled eggs	butter

Slice lengthways, but do not peel, 6 aubergines and let the slices drain. Soften the skinned chopped tomatoes and the chopped onion in a small saucepan with a little oil, mashing up the tomato flesh while you stir.

Give the aubergine slices a final drain by pressing them between your hands, coat them thinly with flour, put them into a shallow pan with hot oil, and let them colour to pale brown.

Grease a fireproof dish and put half the tomato sauce at the bottom. Then comes a layer of aubergine, followed by egg, then sliced cheese. Repeat these layers for a second time, finishing with tomato. Sprinkle with grated cheese, dot with butter, and bake for 20 minutes in a medium oven.

Baking & Eggs

Vegetable and pastry are natural allies. Under a baked crust, in a baked case, or on a baked bed, vegetables at once become a substantial course, and little else is needed, except for perhaps some soup and cheese, to make a satisfying meal. The Russians serve *piroshki*, savoury cabbage-filled puff-pastry parcels, with their clear vegetable soups; the French dish up any number of flans and tarts (of which the *Quiche lorraine* is merely the best-known example) with a green salad. Cornishmen have Cornish pasties – large triangles filled with a mixture of potato, onions and meat; and in Italy there are endless pizzas – fat circles of dough, crisp on the outside and fluffy within, topped with tomato mush and mozzarella cheese and decorated with anchovies and olives. This is not to mention the little *bateaux* and minute *bouchées*, filled with asparagus, mushrooms and so on, encountered at drinks parties, nor the large, puffy vol-au-vents which are often served at formal dinners.

The basic pastry may be puff, short, or yeast-proven. The first two can be bought, in bags or frozen, ready to roll out; but usually, although they take time to make, short pastry is shorter, and puff pastry is puffier, if it is homemade.

Shortcrust pastry

4oz (110g; ½ cup) fat (lard or butter – ideally, half and half)

8oz (225g) plain flour
salt
2–3 tablespoons water

Cut the fat into dice, and rub it with your fingertips into the sifted flour, to which you have added a pinch of salt until you have a mixture that looks like breadcrumbs.

Then using a palette knife and 2–3 tablespoons water, work the crumbly mixture until you have a ball of stiff dough. On a thinly floured surface, as quickly and as lightly as possible, roll out the pastry. Put it into the baking tin and let it stand in a cool place for a little while before baking; this will prevent it from shrinking in the oven. Bake in a fairly hot oven (Reg 6/400°F) until golden. If you are baking 'blind' – i.e. if the filling is to be added later, fill the pastry-lined tin with pulse or clean pebbles from the garden, so that the sides do not collapse.

Puff pastry

Cold ingredients, a cool rolling surface such as marble, quick handling and a hot oven are what make puff pastry rise to the heights. *Mille feuilles* are the aim – or a crust of perhaps not quite a thousand thin pastry layers with a lot of air in between.

8oz (225g; 1 cup) butter
8oz (225g; 2 cups) plain flour
salt
water

Cut three-quarters of the cold butter into little dice, and add to the sifted, salted flour. Using a palette knife, mix into a dough, adding a couple of spoons of water. Do not worry if the mixture seems lumpy with butter – this is to the good.

Roll out with light, upward strokes to a thickness of about ½in (1cm). Fold into a Z-shape – one-third of the pastry on top, one-third in the middle, one-third below. Using half the remaining butter, put a lump into each of the folds, give the pastry half a turn and roll out again. Repeat this process one more time, put the pastry into a cold place to rest and bake it in a hot oven (Reg 7/425°F).

Pizza dough

1½lb (675g) strong white flour	1 lump sugar
3 teaspoons salt	¾ pint (⅜l; 1½ cups) – or a little less – hand-hot water
1 tablespoon dried yeast or 1oz (25g) compressed fresh yeast	

Put the flour in a warm bowl and mix in the salt. Dissolve the yeast and sugar lump in ¼ pint (⅛l; ½ cup) of the measured water. Put in a warm place until it starts to froth – it is a good idea to warm the flour slightly at the same time.

When the yeast looks frothy and active, pour it into a well in the middle of the flour and add half the remaining liquid; work to a smooth silky dough using as much more water as you need. Knead the dough and then put it, covered with a damp cloth and thickly folded towel, in a warm place to rise for an hour or two until it has doubled in size.

Neapolitan pizza (*3 large ones or 6 small*)

1lb (450g) pizza dough	anchovy fillets
2lb (900g) tomatoes, skinned and chopped	black olives, stoned
1 or 2 mozzarella cheeses	oregano, basil or marjoram
	olive oil

Preheat the oven to Reg 6/400°F. When the dough has risen and been kneaded, shape it into flat rounds or oblongs the size of the pizza you want to make, and lay them in greased tins. Spread liberally with the tomatoes and lay slices of cheese, anchovy fillets and black olives on top. Sprinkle with oregano, basil or marjoram and a generous amount of olive oil – about 1 dessertspoon for each small pizza. Do not take the filling right to the edges, because the crust makes a sort of bank to keep the filling in while it cooks. Leave for 20 minutes to rise again. Bake in a fairly hot oven (Reg 5/375°F) for a further 15–20 minutes.

Sage and onion tart (*for 4*)

4 medium-sized onions, chopped	chopped parsley
knob of butter	1 egg
¼ pint (⅛l; ½ cup) cream	4 rashers streaky bacon, fried
1 tablespoon chopped sage	½lb (225g) shortcrust pastry
salt, pepper	

Sauté the onions in butter, until golden and soft. Mix the ingredients in a bowl and add the onions and the fried bacon cut in strips. Line a tin with pastry and pour in the seasoned mixture. Bake in a fairly hot oven (Reg 6/400°F) for about 20 minutes.

Pissaladière (*for 4–6*)

1½lb (675g) onions,	1lb (450g) very red tomatoes, the riper the better
5 tablespoons olive oil	
salt, pepper	
½lb (225g) shortcrust pastry	1 tin anchovy fillets in oil
	20 small black olives

Slice the onions. Heat the olive oil in a heavy saucepan and soften the onions, cooking them for 30 minutes and turning them gently from time to time so that they colour evenly. They should be golden and translucent. Season them with salt and pepper.

Line a baking sheet with a fairly thin layer of pastry, banking up the edges to form a reservoir for the onions, oil, etc., and cover it with a thick layer of onions. Now add the sliced tomatoes, pressing them down lightly. Lay a lattice of anchovies on top and put an olive in the centre of each lattice.

Sprinkle with more olive oil and bake in a hot oven (Reg 7/425°F) for 15 minutes, then at a lower temperature, (Reg 5/375°F) for 30 minutes. Serve hot or cold.

Spinach tart (*for 3–4*)

2lb (900g) fresh spinach	1oz (25g; ¼ cup) Gruyère cheese, grated
½ pint (¼l; 1 cup) Béchamel sauce	salt, pepper
2 cloves of garlic	½lb (225g) shortcrust pastry

Make the pastry in advance, and chill, then line a flan case with it. Cook the spinach in a covered saucepan with a sprinkling of salt. Make a smooth Béchamel sauce and add the crushed cloves of garlic, salt, pepper and cheese.

Drain the spinach very well for at least 15 minutes. Chop it slightly. Meanwhile bake your tart shell blind for 15–20 minutes. Mix the spinach into the sauce, which should be quite thick as the spinach holds a lot of water. Pour into the flan case. Bake in a hot oven (Reg 6/400°F) for 20 minutes until lightly browned. This is also good eaten cold.

Béchamel (*and Mornay*) sauce

2oz (50g; ¼ cup) butter	½ pint (¼l; 1 cup) milk
2 tablespoons flour	salt, pepper

To make this basic white sauce, which is also the foundation for a soufflé, combine the butter and flour over a gentle heat. Heat the milk in a separate pan, and when it is hot – not boiling – pour it into the butter and flour mixture. Remove the pan from the heat and stir briskly until the sauce is smooth and lumpless. Return the pan to the heat and simmer gently, stirring continuously for about 5 minutes to ensure that the flour gets cooked. (The addition of 3 tablespoons of grated cheese transforms this into a Mornay sauce, which you must beat with a wooden spoon to make velvety.)

Soufflé of root vegetables

1lb (450g) turnips, parsnips or Jerusalem artichokes	$\frac{1}{4}$ pint ($\frac{1}{8}$l; $\frac{1}{2}$ cup) milk
2oz (50g; $\frac{1}{4}$ cup) butter	chopped parsley
3oz (75g; $\frac{3}{4}$ cup) flour	salt, pepper
	4 eggs

Cook the vegetables until they are done, drain well – reserving the water – and mash them into a smooth purée. Make a Béchamel sauce with the butter, flour, milk and $\frac{1}{4}$ pint ($\frac{1}{8}$l; $\frac{1}{2}$ cup) of the reserved vegetable water. Stir in the purée and the parsley, and season to taste. Separate the eggs and beat the yolks into the sauce with the pan off the heat. Whip the egg whites until they stand up in peaks. Stir in a spoonful of the beaten whites, and then fold in the rest gently – it does not matter if an odd blob of white remains. Pour into a buttered 2-pint (1$\frac{1}{2}$l; 4 cup) soufflé dish and cook for 20 minutes in a fairly hot oven (Reg 6/400°F).

Spinach soufflé (*for 4*)

a knob of butter	$\frac{1}{2}$ pint ($\frac{1}{4}$l; 1 cup) Béchamel
1oz (25g) Parmesan cheese	sauce, cooled slightly
6oz (160g) spinach purée	1oz (25g; $\frac{1}{4}$ cup) Gruyère
4 eggs, plus 1 egg white	cheese, grated

Butter a soufflé dish and dust inside with grated Parmesan. Heat the spinach gently in a closed pan with a little butter. Do not fry. Add the egg yolks one by one to the Béchamel sauce, beating them in with a wire whisk. Stir in the spinach purée. Beat the egg whites until stiff, stirring a quarter of them with most of the cheese into the spinach mixture. Fold in the remaining egg whites, turn into the soufflé dish and sprinkle with the rest of the Parmesan and Gruyère cheese. Bake for 25 minutes on the middle shelf of the oven pre-heated to Reg 5/375°F.

Little tomato soufflés (*for 6*)

12 large tomatoes	pepper
1oz (25g; $\frac{1}{4}$ cup) flour	1 tablespoon grated
1oz (25g; $\frac{1}{8}$ cup) butter	Parmesan cheese
1 tablespoon cream	basil
salt	4 eggs, plus 1 egg white

Cut the tops off the tomatoes, scoop out the centres and cook these until reduced by half. Sieve and use this purée to make a Béchamel sauce with the butter and flour. Stir in the cream, salt, pepper, Parmesan and some chopped basil. You may not need all the tomato pulp as the mixture must not be too sloppy. Add the egg yolks one at a time, beating each one in well. Beat the egg whites to a soft light foam. Stir 2 table-spoons of this into the tomato mixture, then add the rest,

folding in carefully. Fill the tomatoes to the top with the mixture. Preheat the oven to Reg 7/425°F. Put in the tomatoes and turn the heat down to Reg 6/400°F and cook for 15–20 minutes, when the soufflés should be well risen.

Pancake batter (*makes about 10 pancakes*)

4oz (110g; 1 cup) plain flour	1 egg
pinch of salt	$\frac{1}{2}$ pint ($\frac{1}{4}$l; 1 cup) milk

Sift the flour and salt into a bowl, add the beaten egg and whisk well until the mixture is smooth. Add half the milk and continue beating. Leave the mixture to stand for a little while before adding the rest of the milk and whisking it once more, until the batter has the consistency of thin cream. Heat a little olive oil in a heavy-based shallow pan – the pan should be really hot – and coat the bottom of the pan with batter, tilting the pan this way and that to spread the mixture. When the underside is cooked and golden, slip the pancake over and cook the other side – each side should take about 1 minute.

Mayonnaise

Homemade mayonnaise is infinitely nicer than even the best bottled sort. Choose a good olive oil; its taste will predominate. For each egg yolk, you will need about $\frac{1}{6}$ pint ($\frac{1}{10}$l; 8 tablespoons) of olive oil. Two yolks and $\frac{1}{3}$ pint ($\frac{1}{6}$l; $\frac{3}{4}$ cup) will give you a reasonable amount for 4 people. You also need 1 teaspoon of white vinegar or lemon juice, some salt, pepper, and 1 teaspoon of French mustard.

Put the egg yolks into a basin and stir them about with the mustard and a pinch of salt. Then, drop by drop and stirring steadily, add the oil. The mixture will quickly become thick and glossy; it will not take more than 3 minutes at the outside. When this has happened, the oil can be added in a thin stream. Add the vinegar or lemon juice when you are about halfway through the operation; this will make the mayonnaise look a little opaque, but it will regain its char-acteristic consistency when you go on adding the oil as before. Continue until the oil is used up, or until the mayonnaise will not absorb any more. Then, you can either stop, or add about 1 teaspoon of tepid water, which will enable it to absorb even more. Should the mayonnaise curdle (and that usually happens only in the initial stages) start again with another yolk, and slowly add the curdled mixture.

Mayonnaise verte

For a 2-egg mayonnaise, mix it with 3–4 tablespoons of greenery: chives, parsley, tarragon, chervil and young spinach leaves pounded into a juicy mush. (This can also be added to Hollandaise sauce to make a warm *Sauce verte*.)

Hollandaise sauce

4oz (110g; $\frac{1}{2}$ cup) butter	1 large egg yolk
1 tablespoon white vinegar	salt, pepper

Cut the butter into small cubes and if it is very hard let it soften a little. Take a double saucepan, or a pan into which a suitable bowl or basin will fit, and heat some water in the bottom to just below boiling point. To lessen the risk of the sauce curdling, keep the water below the boil, and make sure it does not actually touch the base of the bowl or pan in which the sauce is cooking.

Using the bowl or pan which is to go over the water, beat the vinegar with the egg yolk and a cube of the soft butter. Place it over the hot water and, stirring all the time with a wooden spoon, add the cubes of butter one at a time, letting each one melt before you add another.

If the sauce shows signs of thickening too fast, or curdling, remove it at once from over the hot water. If it is too thick, add a few drops of water or top of the milk. Taste for salt. If it is too sharp, add some unsalted butter. It should be smooth and fairly thick, and is served lukewarm.

A tablespoon of whipped cream added just before serving makes this a *Sauce mousseline*. Whipped cream added to mayonnaise makes a *Sauce mousseuse*.

Lemon dressing

1 onion	1 teaspoon tarragon or mint
1 gherkin	4–5 tablespoons oil
1 hard-boiled egg	3 tablespoons lemon juice
1 teaspoon capers	salt

Chop all the solid ingredients as finely as possible and mix with the oil and lemon juice. Season. Use to dress a salad of mixed raw vegetables.

Sauce beurre blanc

2 tablespoons shallots, finely chopped	$\frac{1}{2}$lb (225g) fresh butter
$\frac{1}{3}$ cup vinegar	salt
	pepper

Cook the shallots gently in the vinegar until it has all but evaporated. Remove from the heat, but put in a warm place of even temperature. If no such spot is available in your kitchen, simply return the pan to the heat from time to time – but never let the butter boil. Like mayonnaise, this sauce is a little tricky to make, and has a tendency to go oily. Add the butter bit by bit, whisking constantly, and you end up with a rich creamy sauce.

Timbale (*for 4*)

Timbale really describes the dish in which a kind of savoury pudding or mould is cooked, and it is derived from the Arab word *thabal*, meaning drum.

A true gourmet will expect his timbale to be cooked or served in a pie crust, but ordinary domestic timbale cases are made in fireproof porcelain the same shape and colour as the real thing.

For a hot carrot timbale, melt 1 tablespoon of butter in a thick pan and gently cook about 2 cups of finely sliced carrots for about 10 minutes. Add enough stock or water to cover the carrots and cook them until they are quite soft. Drain well and sieve into a purée. Whisk 1 egg and add to it 1 slightly beaten egg white and the carrot purée, and season well.

Butter a timbale case or 4 individual moulds and decorate the bottom of the mould with a slice of hard-boiled egg. Fill the case or moulds two-thirds full, cover with greaseproof paper, and place in a pan of hot water, to bake in a moderate oven for 45 minutes.

Turn out and serve hot with a Béchamel sauce.

Egg and lemon sauce

2 eggs	juice of $\frac{1}{2}$ lemon
salt, pepper	$\frac{1}{4}$ pint ($\frac{1}{8}$l; $\frac{1}{2}$ cup) stock

Separate the eggs. Beat the whites until stiff, then combine them with the yolks and a little salt and pepper in the top of a double boiler, or over a pan of hot water. Squeeze the lemon and add the juice to the eggs a few drops at a time, alternating with a few drops of stock, and whisking as you go.

Do not let the water in the bottom of the double boiler touch the top pan, but it can simmer without spoiling the sauce, it is a light, delicately flavoured, primrose-coloured foam.

Sauce rémoulade

1 hard-boiled egg	tarragon, chives, parsley
1 raw egg yolk	1 gherkin, chopped finely
1 teaspoon lemon juice	1 shallot, chopped
$\frac{1}{4}$ pint ($\frac{1}{8}$l; $\frac{1}{2}$ cup) olive oil	1 teaspoon capers

Pound the yolk and chop the white of the hard-boiled egg into minute pieces; add a few drops of lemon juice. Mix the raw yolk, and proceed as for mayonnaise. Finally stir in the herbs, the chopped gherkin, shallot and the capers.

Picnics

Simplicity and ease of eating are the watchwords for picnics, since all food tastes better out of doors anyway, and complicated meals *al fresco* should be left to those well equipped with butlers and other comforts. Picnic food should be easy to control with fingers and the minimum of tools, and it should not fall about. Hence the tradition of sandwiches and pastry cases containing endless combinations of meat, cheese and fruit which could well be augmented with vegetables.

Whether you are in dappled glades by running water, having sand blown between your teeth at the seaside, or sheltering and shivering in a convenient cave, picnic food must taste fresh and be appetizing.

All sorts of salads can be carried in plastic jars and cups; vacuum flasks keep thin, iced consommé-type soups cool in the heat, or warming broths piping hot, if you are keen on eating in the snow. Pasties and their like and all sorts of quiches are good; and bread figures largely – crusty French bread if possible. The flat Greek type, or wholemeal, rye bread or rolls or buns are also good, and can be stuffed with a variety of fillings.

Pan bania (*the archetypal picnic food*)

French loaf	12 small black olives
6 spring onions	small tin anchovies in
1 green or red pepper	olive oil
4 tomatoes	2 hard-boiled eggs

Cut the French loaf lengthways. Cut the onions into thin slices, cut the pepper in strips. Peel the tomatoes and cut them into manageable pieces. Mix all the ingredients, except the eggs, with your best Vinaigrette dressing, using the oil from the anchovies plus extra olive oil, and allow to stand for an hour or two. Add the sliced eggs at this stage, and pile the mixture into French bread and wrap in foil.

Another method of making *pan bania* is to rub the cut surface of the bread with garlic before putting in the filling, and placing the giant sandwich under a heavy weight for about 1 hour. You could also scoop out the crumb, and mix it into the filling; then pile it back into the hollow crusts.

Alternative cold, raw fillings

Any number of other salad fillings can also be used: Thin slices of raw mushrooms, with lemon juice, crushed garlic, olive oil, and ground black pepper. Chopped parsley mixed in, or green fennel leaves, or marjoram. (As all these fillings are made with oil, butter has no place in the sandwich.)

Niçoise: lettuce hearts, tomato slices, green pepper slices, cucumber and crushed garlic with olive oil and salt and pepper.

Sliced cucumber, chopped chives and mint, seasoned and mixed with a little yoghourt or olive oil – a little cottage or cream cheese is good with this.

Dandelion leaves or sorrel, with chopped shallots or mild onion, chives and garlic, seasoned. This, like similar salads with lettuce or raw spinach, is delicious with some crumbled, cooked bacon sprinkled over it.

Greek lettuce: to strips of crisp fresh lettuce, add sliced spring onions and chopped dill. Season with salt and a little oil and lemon juice.

Finely chopped celery with chopped watercress or land cress, lamb's lettuce, crushed garlic, chopped parsley, stoned black olives and slices of tomato, mixed with oil and lemon dressing with a little grated orange peel added.

Chopped lettuce, watercress, tomatoes, hard-boiled eggs, avocado pear, with crumbled blue cheese, some chopped cold chicken and crumbled fried bacon. All mixed with French dressing.

Some pieces of cold turkey or chicken, with finely chopped onion, green pepper, celery mixed with a little cream and salad dressing with a little curry.

Finely shredded white cabbage, with diced red apples; chopped green pepper and spring onions, a few lamb's lettuce leaves and sultanas, in a mayonnaise or cream dressing.

Sweet red peppers, finely sliced, with tomato and raw broad beans.

These mixtures need not always be sandwiched in bread, but could be eaten straight from a jar, scooped up with crispbread by ardent slimmers. This also applies to the following *pan bania* fillings made with cold cooked vegetables:

Broad beans, cooked, with lemon juice and the yolks of 2 eggs, made into a thick sauce and cooled.

Beetroots, cooked, in the bread buttered with chives, garlic and a little lemon juice mixed with the butter.

Sorrel purée (melt the sorrel in butter and mix with a little cream or Béchamel sauce), makes a good filling. Even better in an omelette, and the whole thing put between the bread slices.

Spinach, Swiss chard, zucchini and chopped onions sautéed in olive oil, with tuna or anchovies added when cold.

Drained cooked spinach added to sliced cold potatoes and slivers of cheese, mixed with a little cream and the juice of a lemon.

Cold boiled haricot beans, mixed while still warm with a little oil and vinegar, chopped onion or shallot, chopped parsley and salami sausage or crumbled, crisply fried bacon. All these vegetables and salad mixtures could be followed by cheese, to be eaten with crunchy celery and radishes – pink and white, red and white, or plain iridescent scarlet – with their clean sharp taste.

RADISH *raphanus sativus*

A bowl of crisp red radishes makes a delicious and decorative addition to any meal. To keep them crisp, or to freshen up a tired bunch, keep them in a bowl of water in the 'fridge. Most people will like them served with plenty of salt and some eat them greenery and all, which makes them less peppery.

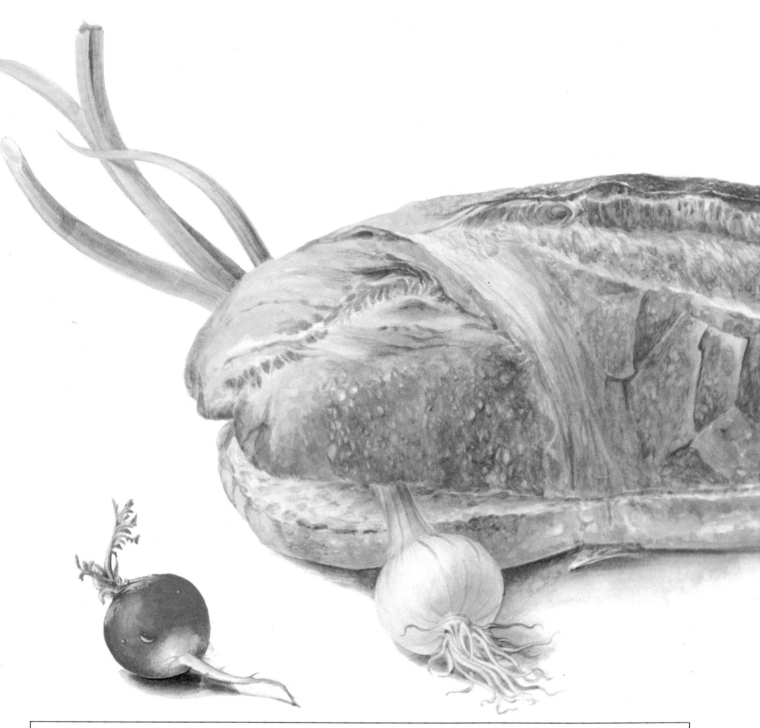

How to grow radishes

Some of the quickest of all seeds to germinate and produce, and, therefore, like lettuces, can be sown between rows of slender germinating vegetables in order to mark the spot. Sow thinly in shallow drills and thin the seedlings early. To be good they must be grown quickly, and this means a lot of watering. They are sown in succession, little and often, from spring to late summer, and prefer a cool, moist spot in the heat of summer. Their obliging speed to show and grow make them firm favourites for childrens' gardens. Large, rooted, winter varieties can be left in the ground until required, and can be eaten raw or cooked like turnips.

1. Draw shallow drills with the teeth of a rake and sow thinly

2. Exhibition growers put radishes under glass, but for eating this is not necessary

Preserving

No vegetable tastes as nice as one that is picked and eaten straight away. But people who grow vegetables have too many at some time in the year and too few at another.

Of course, vegetables like parsnips, leeks, and Jerusalem artichokes can be left in the ground until needed. So can celery and celeriac, although they will need protection with straw in very cold weather. But everything else must be picked and it is only reasonable to preserve the harvest glut for a time of shortage.

With the advent of deep-freezers, some of the old and tried ways have suffered a decline, but unless a very large home-freezer is available, the older methods are still useful.

It is still a pleasure, on Christmas Eve, to unearth a large biscuit tin or some such container, filled with new potatoes which, after lifting, had been buried in the summer. The potatoes will have remained miraculously new and are much nicer than frozen ones to go with the turkey. And it is very little bother (and rather space-saving) to store the main-crop potatoes, and late varieties of roots, which should be allowed to mature before harvesting, in outdoor clamps.

If you store your potatoes indoors, you must put them into sacks. These should be folded over to keep out the light.

Plaits of onions and garlic, hanging in a cool, dry, airy place indoors can almost bridge the gap between the last crop and the new, and for the in-between period, it is highly convenient to have in store a jar with dried onion rings. Marrows can be hung up in nets, and should there be a surplus of mushrooms (which there hardly ever is because they are so delicious eaten fresh) it is the simplest thing in the world to string them up – like a pearl necklace, to which occasional additions are made – and to dry them for future use. The seeds of overgrown beans can be transformed into home-made pulse.

Salting – once the most popular method of preserving green beans – produces a taste of its own. This is only slightly related to that of a fresh bean, but is liked by many people.

Bottling is a highly satisfactory activity. Like baking bread, it makes one feel virtuous and provident, and even if freezing is superior in preserving the true taste of most vegetables it is a pity to take up freezer space with tomatoes destined for soup. They might just as well be bottled, and besides, a row of shiny glass jars with the contents visible tends to lift the heart. This also applies to pickling. Incidentally, bottles and jars, neatly labelled and wearing Mother Hubbard caps, make excellent Christmas presents.

Drying

The advantage of drying is that it can be carried out intermittently, and in a variety of locations. The airing cupboard, the opened oven as it cools after having been in use for other purposes, the area above a radiator or boiler are all suitable for this purpose. Whether you spread out your vegetables on a cake-rack, string them on cords or thin canes, or simply use ordinary trays (on which the things to be dried must be turned

every now and then), all you need is warm air and ventilation. Half a minute's blanching is advisable for onion rings, sliced fleshy runner beans, and shelled broad beans. Overgrown beans, peas and haricots should be left on the vine until the pods have become yellow. Then shuck them and dry the seeds. Late crops can be pulled up and hung to dry in their entirety, and shelled afterwards. The only thing to remember is that *slow* drying gives the best results.

Salting

Runner beans (and, of course, cabbage for choucroute) are the only vegetables suitable for salting.

For the beans, kitchen (not refined) salt should be used, in the proportion of 1lb (450g) salt to 3lb (1½kg) beans. Put the beans and salt in alternate layers in a glass or stoneware jar (not a metal one), starting and ending with salt and filling up every few days as the beans shrink. By the time the jar is full the salt will have formed a brine (which is what preserves the beans). Cover tightly. Take out in the quantities required, wash well in several waters, and soak in warm water for 2 hours. Cook in boiling water without salt.

Bottling

This operation needs special care and equipment – a reliable step-by-step guidebook is a necessary investment, and so is a pressure cooker, now that the traditional kilner jars are getting very hard to come by.

Although green vegetables inevitably lose much of their colour when preserved by this method, and the addition of green artificial colouring is sometimes advised, there is a good deal to be said for the pale delicate colouring of bottled green peas, provided they have been picked while they are tiny. The same cannot be said for green beans – the loss of colour makes them look faded and old. But cauliflower bottles well, as does asparagus; and carrots look nice, fresh and cheerful.

The vegetables should be prepared and blanched as for freezing, and packed – not too tightly – into the sterilized jars while still hot. Add a little salt and top up the jars, to within ½in (1cm) of the top, with the blanching liquid. Clamp the lids on lightly and place the jars in the pressure cooker. Steam at the standard recommended pressure.

Pickling

Red cabbage, cauliflower, mushrooms, onions and green tomatoes (as well as nasturtium seeds) can be pickled, since the marinade in which they are kept preserves them. The prepared vegetables are normally sprinkled with salt, or if they have a high water content, are placed in brine. After 12–48 hours they are drained, thoroughly washed if they have been in salt, packed into jars and covered with cold spiced vinegar. For the vinegar, put into a large basin 2 pints (1¼l) of vinegar, ¼oz (5g) cinnamon bark, ¼oz (5g) cloves, ¼oz (5g) allspice, and a few peppercorns (the spices should, if possible, be whole). Cover the basin, put it in a saucepan of water and bring to the boil. Remove, and strain and use the vinegar when it is cold.

To pickle beetroot, you need to cook it until it is tender. Then skin and dice, pack into jars within 2 fingers of the top, and cover with the spiced vinegar, close, label and store.

Gherkins need to be steeped in brine, drained, patted dry and packed into a jar. The spiced vinegar is then poured over them, and the jar closed and left for 24 hours in a warm place. After this time, drain off the vinegar, boil it up, and pour it back over the gherkins, leaving it for another 24 hours. The gherkins will go greener with every new drenching, so you can repeat the process until they have assumed the shade you like. Then top up with more vinegar, cork and store.

Freezing

Nearly all vegetables freeze well, especially beans of all kinds, Brussels sprouts, carrots, cauliflower, sprouting broccoli, leeks, mushrooms, peas and spinach. But do not freeze salad vegetables, which go soggy when they thaw. The vegetables should be cleaned and prepared in the usual way, and then blanched. Blanching times are given opposite. These show the times from when the water comes to the boil after the vegetables have been put in. After blanching, plunge into cold water, drain, pat dry, and freeze in small quantities. Properly prepared frozen vegetables can keep in condition for 6–9 months. (Indeed, they can keep longer, but from the point of view of enjoyment, one needs a gap between the last of the frozen and the first of the fresh.) Apart from corn on the cob, which should be allowed to thaw out before cooking, prepare your block of frozen vegetables for the table by putting them halfway up into boiling water.

Jerusalem artichokes, cucumbers and marrows – all watery vegetables – should be cooked before freezing. Like aubergines and red cabbage, they are best frozen as part of cooked dishes ready for eating (vegetable ragouts, etc.). Cook them about 15 minutes less than you would normally do, as they will have a second cooking after freezing.

Vegetables	Freezing		Bottling		Salting	Drying	Pickling
	suitability	blanching time (in minutes)	suitability	steaming times (in minutes)	suitability	suitability	suitability
Artichokes, globe							*
Artichokes, Jerusalem	*	(cook)					
Asparagus, thick	*	4	*	35			
thin	*	2					
Aubergines	*	(cook)					
Beans, broad	**	2				*	
French	**	2	*	35		*	
Runner	**	2	*	35	*	*	
Beetroot			*	35		*	*
Brussels Sprouts	**	2					
Cabbage					*		*
Cabbage, red	*	(cook)					*
Carrots	**	3	*	35		*	
Cauliflower	**	2					*
Celeriac	*	4					
Celery, hearts	*	3–4	*	30			
sticks	*	2	*	30			
Corn on the Cob	*	4–6					
Courgettes	*	1					
Cucumber	*	(cook)					
Curly Kale	*	2					
Leeks whole	**	3–4					
in slices	**	2					
Marrows	*	(cook)					*
Mushrooms, button	**	4	*	35			*
flat						*	
Onions						*	*
Peas	**	1	*	40		*	
Peppers	*	2–4					
Potatoes						*	
Spinach	**	2					
Sprouting broccoli	**	2					
Tomatoes	*		*	10			
Tomatoes, juice or purée	*		*	10			
Vegetable macédoine	*		*	40			

Growing a still-life

Go out into the garden with a basket or wooden trug, cut or pick some of your own produce, and immediately there is the sort of still-life the Old Masters used to paint. True, they did not lavish the same sort of attention on vegetables as they gave to fruit and flowers, but carrots, onions, leeks and artichokes (especially artichokes) feature in all sorts of art. Vegetables appear as attributes of Italian Madonnas. Ingeniously arranged, they make Arcimboldo's grotesque portraits with garlic cheeks and corncob ears. In seventeenth- and eighteenth-century paintings, artichokes sit in baroque

silver platters and, when genre pictures came into their own, humbler vegetables began to spill from baskets onto kitchen floors.

Very often at horticultural shows, after reeling with astonishment and delight at sight of the gorgeously coloured and incredibly large examples of the flower-grower's art, our eyes turn with gratitude to those wonderful pyramids and obelisks of vegetables. Dramatic and decorative, they give inspiration for table-centres: after all, groups of fruit and vegetables were fashioned in the eighteenth century by many of the great porcelain factories.

So do not hide your harvest away – put the vegetables in the kitchen in a basket or wicker tray, or in bowls or just in heaps on the working top, and you have the best sort of decoration. This is of course transitory, until the vegetables are prepared, cooked and eaten, but what pleasure they give; it is suddenly obvious that a cabbage or a cauliflower is just as beautiful as a rose.

For more permanent decoration you will have strings of onions and garlic, or even red chillies, and bunches of herbs, hung up on walls or suspended from the ceiling.

If you have room, a group of the pumpkin and marrow family, ripe and dry, will sit around looking dramatic – green and yellow and orange, plain and striped. You can also grow the ornamental gourds which come in a mixture of bizarre shapes, sizes and colours, and look good as the focal point on a table. There are also the dried cobs of ornamental maize in its purple-to-yellow colour permutations. With these you should have bunches of ornamental grasses, dried, and everlasting flowers like Helichrysums and Acrocliniums, alone or grouped with gleanings from the edges of fields of corn and barley. The dried seed heads of the umbelliferous herbs like fennel and lovage and dill, and the largest and most ornamental of all – angelica – are essentials for decoration. Even the dried heads of carrot flowers and yarrow, and the ball-like heads of onion and leek which have gone to seed, make elegant objects in jugs and jars (although, of course, no self-respecting gardener would allow these vegetables to go to seed; perhaps a few can be left in a corner for drying to use for decoration). Green peppers and aubergines are pretty in bowls or baskets, and a huge dried sunflower head looks splendid on a wall.

Round about Hallowe'en time the pumpkins will really come into their own, when you take out the flesh to make delicious soups, as the skins can be cut into happily smiling faces lit up from within with nightlights or candles. Glowing orange, these are a marvellous decoration indoors and out, and stay dry for a long time. Or they could be cut into tri-angular and crescent shapes to make a beautiful lamp for use at Christmas.

Some people who take over valuable garden space from flowers and shrubs to grow vegetables may be sad at the loss of beauty in favour of use and health, but few people perhaps realize how beautiful vegetables are. The

How to grow corn

Corn, *zea mays*, is not difficult to grow, although it needs a warm, sunny site well out of the wind. Seeds are sown under glass at the end of the spring two to a pot. They are singled to the fittest and planted out with 15in (38cm) between them. Corn always prefers to be planted as if in a field, in a group or a block instead of a row, because it helps fertilization. Seeds can of course also be sown in the open in summer, but the seedlings must be protected from the birds. Ornamental corn should be allowed to ripen on the plant, but sweet corn for eating is better picked young before the great silken tassels turn colour too much. Eat it when the grain is still primrose-yellow and the tops juicy, and don't spare the butter.

There are all sorts of recipes for preparing corn dishes, but unless you grow acres of the stuff it really seems a pity to waste home-grown cobs by stripping off the corn in any other way than by one's own teeth.

1. If no greenhouse is available, corn can be started off by a sunny window

2. Seedlings should go in 15in (40cm) apart

3. Hoeing should be shallow and watering thorough in dry weather

4. Corn should be harvested as and when the individual cobs are ripe

nice thing about vegetable gardens and patches is (or should be) their orderliness – straight lines, neatness, space between the rows for picking; the kind of regimental array which is quite rightly frowned upon in the flower garden. What could be more beautiful than a screen of beans in flower, or a group of tasselled sweetcorn, or a pot of tomatoes – yellow flowers, green and red fruit – or a row of flowering broad beans: surely one of the most beautiful of vegetables looked at as decorative plants. Seakale beet has dramatic leaves and silver mid-ribs good enough for any border; and all the cabbage tribe take some beating as eye-catching plants, with red cabbage perhaps being the star of the show. Any artichokes left uneaten to flower are splendid plants with their silvery leaves, and the large heads may be cut and dried for large-scale flower arrangements.

Living vegetables indoors

Indoor vegetables need as much space between them as outdoor ones, and crowding results in meagre spindly specimens.

All vegetables, even the humble potato, are decorative vegetables in their own right, and most can be grown in pots and tubs, on sills near windows, and on balconies.

The main thing to remember is that a large pot is needed, plus lots of water; water is lost more quickly from pots than from the open ground, because it evaporates both from the surface and the sides of a porous container. Plants grown in confined conditions also need a certain amount of feeding. Never make the mistake of packing too many seedlings or seeds into the pot or box.

It is not a very good idea to experiment with any of the cabbage family or the roots which require a great depth of soil. Carrots for frond decoration are best produced by saving the tops of those you prepare for the kitchen, and placing them, cut surface down, in a saucer with a little water. (This, together with mustard and cress, makes a good introduction to gardening for children, as results are so fast.) But a sprouting potato, put into a bucket or tin filled with compost, and earthed up like one grown in the wide open spaces, will produce handsome foliage, star-shaped flowers, and delicious little new potatoes as well.

Any large container will do, provided it has drainage holes; so, decorative as the plant is, it should not be put directly into a hole-less ornamental container.

Lettuces are so quick to come to maturity that they are a must for the window-box gardener. There are many small varieties which are very suitable for the purpose; and it is a good idea to arrange for a continuous supply by keeping some in a 'nursery pot', from which seedlings can be transplanted into the main box to replace those which are eaten.

Tomatoes and beans are natural pot subjects, as both grow upwards and take little valuable horizontal space. Both like the sun, and both need vertical support: put in the canes with the plants. See that they never dry out. Tomatoes come in minature varieties – small fruit but many of them provided that side shoots are regularly pinched out. Seedlings need 8in (20cm) pots. When sowing beans, allow 3 seeds to a 12in (30cm) pot, spaced round the periphery. (Pessimists allow 2 seeds per station, singling out to the strongest shoot when germination has taken place.) A pretty way of growing them is on 3 sticks tied together at the top, so that you have a green flowering and fruiting obelisk.

Index

PDO 83-1054